I0816260

Mindful Soldier

Mindful Soldier

Building Resilience to Overcome Life's Challenges

Ash Alexander-Cooper OBE
with Dr Jessica K Miller

QUERCUS

First published in Great Britain in 2026 by Quercus
Part of John Murray Group

2

A CIP catalogue record for this book is available from the British Library

HB ISBN 978 1 52945 064 4
TPB ISBN 978 1 52945 065 1
EBOOK ISBN 978 1 52945 066 8

Typeset in Minion by CC Book Production

Printed in the United States of America

Papers used by Quercus are from well-managed forests and other responsible sources.

Quercus
Carmelite House
50 Victoria Embankment
London EC4Y 0DZ

John Murray Group
Part of Hodder & Stoughton Limited
An Hachette UK company

The authorised representative in the EEA is Hachette Ireland,
8 Castlecourt Centre, Dublin 15, D15 XTP3, Ireland (email: info@hbgi.ie)

‘Between stimulus and response there is a space. And in that space is our power to choose our response and, in that response, lies our growth and our freedom.’

Viktor Frankl, Auschwitz survivor,
in *Man’s Search for Meaning*, 1946

Contents

Author's Note

The fact that I am writing an author's note feels surreal: becoming an author was not something I had planned at all. Although my life has been filled with an abundance of challenge, adversity, adventure and excitement, I didn't for a moment think that these experiences, or the ways in which I have overcome the more traumatic aspects of them, would be worthy of a book. However, with friends and clients alike telling me that they have been inspired by my stories of resilience, that they have found them to be helpful and motivating, and that they'd love to hear more, I've been encouraged to write. So, here we are!

Only a lucky few navigate life without trauma: the majority of us face challenges that leave scars: some physical, others mental. Yet, despite the likelihood we will experience trauma at some point, most of us are ill-equipped to deal effectively with it. By sharing some of my experiences and arming you with some practical advice for overcoming adversity, building resilience and overcoming life's toughest obstacles, I hope that you may be better able to face your own challenges with confidence.

While much of this book is the product of my personal and professional experience, it benefits in large part from the expertise of Dr Jess Miller. It is her neuropsychological knowledge that transforms my lived experience into meaningful skills, tools and techniques; elements that I hope you – the reader – will find useful. To that end, we have included simple practical exercises addressing core themes and, for those who have a deeper interest in the research around trauma and resilience, after each exercise, Jess digs into the 'Science and Thinking' of the psychology covered in each chapter. To create a cohesive narrative, I have written the text in a single voice, but where psychological insights are captured in my narrative, I want to give due credit for Jess' input.

There are many scenes, stories and examples of a personal or otherwise sensitive nature in this book. To protect the privacy of individuals, names and identifying details have been changed or removed. I have endeavoured to do so in a way that does not fundamentally alter the truth of the experiences I relate – nor what is to be learned from them. Additionally, the locations and details of some of the military operations featured have been redacted to protect the security of those involved and the operating procedures of British and other coalition forces.

I hope very much that you will find this an interesting, entertaining, but above all helpful and inspiring read. And, even if you don't, remember that I am donating all author's profits to two veterans' charities, namely Royal British Legion Industries (RBLI) and The Gurkha Welfare Trust (GWT), who do so much to provide mental and physical support to those most in need as a result of their service.

1

Bees and Bullets

Learning to Adapt When Things Don't Go to Plan

'In the midst of chaos, there is also opportunity.'

Sun Tzu, Chinese strategist and philosopher, in *The Art of War*

This was a day when everything went horribly wrong.

It was Halloween, but rather than spending the evening trick-or-treating with family and friends back home, I found myself, dressed in combat clothing and body armour, sweating profusely, preparing for a complex military night operation.

Intelligence suggested that our target was responsible for coordinating the construction of hundreds of improvised explosive devices (IEDs) that had, for months, been responsible for indiscriminate carnage and loss of life. Although I didn't consciously make the connection at the time, an ability to recognise a higher purpose being at stake can be an effective way to prime the brain when dealing with immediate threats.

That night's plan saw my team travel to a coalition outpost near the bombmaker's home, which doubled as a factory. From this temporary forward operating base, we would move to the target under cover of darkness, to carry out what we hoped would be a speedy operation. The route would take us along a newly constructed motorway, since abandoned by an increasingly wary civilian population and now littered with the twisted carcasses of burned-out vehicles – evidence of recent insurgent activity and a salutary reminder that the threat to life was real.

Travelling in unarmoured open-top vehicles gave us excellent manoeuvrability and visibility, but left us both exposed and vulnerable to attack from every angle by a wily and enterprising enemy.

Following a nerve-wracking, but thankfully uneventful, transit we reached the dusty coalition base just a few miles from where we hoped our target would be. There, we met up with a coalition unit tasked with supporting our mission, with whom we had a close working relationship.

After delivering a set of confirmatory orders, during which the mechanics of the mission were outlined – including several contingency plans should things go awry – we carried out last-minute equipment checks before rolling out towards the target.

I glanced at my watch. It was just before midnight.

Although late, much of the heat from the day remained and, as our vehicles bounced along potholed streets piled high with household waste, the warm night air was thick with the sickly scent of decay.

The drive was short. In less than ten minutes we arrived in the vicinity of the bombmaker's house, now illuminated by infrared lasers; dancing green lights visible only with night vision goggles (NVGs).

Dismounting our vehicles as silently as possible, we began to secure the area around the compound in which we hoped we would find our man, in order to prevent unwanted vehicles or people encroaching as the mission progressed. Our coalition partners would clear the buildings on one side of the street as we took responsibility for those on the other.

Once all teams confirmed that the cordon was in place, we made entry to building number 37, as identified on the gridded satellite map I'd attached to my wrist for ease of reference.

Given the fact that our target was believed to be prolific in terms of his links to IEDs, suicide bombers and trafficking fighters, we had to move deliberately and carefully for fear of inadvertently detonating defensive booby traps, whose presence had become increasingly common.

Such caution was justified.

Although buildings 35 and 36 were clear, we hit the jackpot at number 37.

No sooner had the lead team entered through the main gate than they located a vehicle containing a fully constructed IED loaded casually in the back.

As was the trend at the time, this IED specialist had taken an old artillery shell and encased it in a concrete mould, the intention being that it would resemble an ordinary kerbstone for a sidewalk, which could then be positioned at the side of the road. So placed, insurgents would camouflage it with rubbish and other detritus before retreating to a safe distance. From there they could detonate devices safely, using command wire or remote control, as soon as an unsuspecting security or coalition force convoy or rival insurgent group drove past.

Either through overconfidence, carelessness or perhaps inexperience, not only had the bomber made no attempt to conceal the bomb, other than partially covering it with a small, dirty rag, but he'd also left two yellow wires protruding from the concrete casing, making it obvious even to the untrained eye that this was an IED. Although the night was young, with the potential for many things still to go wrong, this early success gave us confidence that we were on the right path and the small spike in our feel-good dopamine at this stage in the mission gave us a welcome boost; something I've since learned to train myself to seek out and make a bigger part of my daily routine – something we can all do, and a theme we pick up on this later in the book.

The team checked that there was no obvious or immediate danger from the device itself (the bomb had not been connected to a power source) and proceeded to the house, within which we could see the dim glow of a lamp.

Forcing the front door to gain entry to the main living area, we found a family eating at the kitchen table.

As the lead team member rapidly scanned the room, the emerging picture was not exactly what you would call normal.

Although obviously a family home, the house clearly doubled up as a bomb factory: IED-making paraphernalia littered almost every surface. For the bombmaker, apparently, leaving grenades, fuses and detonators lying around, all within reach of small children, was not an issue.

Whether or not the adult male was the bombmaker or just a member of the insurgent network, he put up no resistance. After processing and collecting other key personal details, we passed him to the local coalition unit, who took him away for further questioning. This handover allowed us to stay focused on the remainder of our task, without distraction. In neuropsychological terms, I have learned that this constitutes what is known as a 'safety cue', something that allows the brain to mark one threat as being over and to move on to preparing for the next. Something I would become quite familiar with during my army career.

We now had a decision to make: either accept this as the end of a successful mission – which it was – or press on and clear the remainder of the street, with a view to gleaning additional information about the local dynamics and potentially valuable intelligence about other insurgent activity in the area?

Given that we'd made such an effort and taken some risk to drive all that way, as well as having managed to assemble a potent package of ground- and air-support assets, all of which remained on station to support us, we decided to stay a little longer and see what else we could unearth.

Adapting the plan on the fly, we split the group into several smaller teams and began to patrol the remainder of the still empty target street, knocking on doors and chatting to (rather than formally questioning) the families living there.

As we moved methodically from house to house, we found that all the occupants claimed to have neither knowledge of nor affiliation to any insurgent groups: no surprise there. Despite our scepticism about the veracity of such claims, we found no incriminating evidence to suggest otherwise, so we kept moving.

While some dwellings showed signs of life, with shafts of light spilling out onto dusty courtyards and gardens, or the chatter of children playing inside, others gave little or nothing away, apart from the occasional low growl or angry bark from a dog chained up or lurking somewhere within.

Having cleared house number 18, my team of five leapfrogged another group to move onto building 22, an imposing compound with high stone walls and a solid-looking metal gate.

As I strained to peer through the small hole in the centre, through which a padlocked chain was threaded, I could see nothing obvious to suggest that anyone might be inside. The fact that it had been secured from the outside gave us further cause to believe that the place was indeed empty.

The compound was larger than most on the street, effectively a double plot, with an open area immediately to the front and side of the main house, which took up the left half of the walled perimeter. The building itself was an imposing structure, spread over two floors, with columns supporting a roof terrace extending several feet out from the first floor.

Apart from random piles of bricks and other building materials in the garden, this had all the hallmarks of a plot still under construction; in other words, an empty compound that should not take too long for us to clear.

However, whoever owned it, clearly didn't want anyone snooping around; the large padlock was evidence of that.

Despite using bolt cutters to remove the main barrier to entry, the gate remained stubbornly closed, unwilling to admit us. Instead, we turned to the crowbar for a second attempt, but with my colleague Chris struggling to gain enough purchase, I resorted to kicking the now straining metal. This did the trick and the right-hand panel sprung open far enough to reveal, in hazy green hues through my NVGs, the dusty, rubbish-strewn courtyard.

Without additional commands being issued or needed, the team moved quickly through the gap: Chris and Paul to the left, Ed moving in and to the right. I was just behind them, with Mike bringing up the rear, on my right shoulder.

We pressed forward and left, towards the front of the main building, all the while scanning for potential threats.

So far so good.

Then, just as I glanced up to the roof, all hell broke loose. If there was any shouting before the shooting started, I certainly didn't hear it.

The first thing I saw at that moment was what appeared to be a swarm of orange, stinging bees flying towards us. Of course, they weren't bees (which would have been preferable) but bullets – hundreds of bullets raining down from the roof on me and my team from multiple machine guns.

Although we didn't know it then, far from being a deserted dwelling, we had inadvertently stumbled across a house packed with fighters who were undergoing training, before being trafficked to other parts of the country to carry out their own attacks.

Very much a 'trick' rather than a 'treat' kind of welcome from the occupants of number 22.

We would later learn that some of the insurgents decided to escape as they saw us approach, but the majority who remained were determined to fight and had positioned themselves on the roof to do just that, no more than 20 or 30 feet from us. Thanks to their commanding position above us, they had an excellent view of the courtyard below into which they were firing with everything at their disposal.

Frustratingly, and unlike many other firefights in which I found myself later in my career, far from time slowing down on this occasion, everything happened very much in a blur.

To say it came as a shock would be an understatement: this was like nothing I had ever experienced in my life, and it all felt very out of control.

Having made our way just inside the high compound walls as the first bullets were fired, we were placed perfectly in the killing zone – the most opportune ground into which one seeks to bring weapons to bear during a pre-planned ambush – with no immediate cover and very few options for escape, other than out of the partially open gate through which we had just entered.

As the leading 'bees' reached us, things were not looking good, but the enemy fighters made an already confusing situation worse when they began firing rocket-propelled grenades (RPGs) in our direction as well. The other coalition unit, now watching the situation unfold from neighbouring roofs where they had taken up overwatch positions to observe the surrounding area, had assumed that we must have triggered a booby trap on making entry.

With the high-explosive warheads travelling at around 600 miles per hour, the first we knew of these weapons being added to the mix was when they exploded on the compound wall behind us, peppering me and my teammates with boiling hot, razor-sharp shrapnel and kicking up yet more dust and dirt.

A split-second later, I was 'stung' several times by bees unleashed in a long burst of automatic fire.

I am occasionally asked what it feels like to be shot.

Although fired upon many times in later incidents, this was the only occasion during my army career when I was physically wounded by gunfire, so it remains my only point of reference, but one that is seared in my consciousness. Even now, I can still picture the scene vividly and remember the same feelings I had at that moment, as if it was yesterday.

In those first confusing seconds I didn't register that I had been hit, let alone with a bullet in each leg. Rather, I felt a mixture of sensations that I had never before experienced and which my brain was unable to process satisfactorily in the moment.

What I felt initially and most acutely was the sense of being winded, as the force of the bullets knocked me backwards through the gate and into the street, where I fell awkwardly, weighed down by my equipment.

Over and above the shock of finding myself in an ambush, the most intense feelings were of nauseating blunt trauma, combined with a strange sense that I had blocked or disrupted the path of objects travelling at considerable speed. Combined with this was a burning, stinging sensation from the grenade shrapnel now buried in my arms and legs, as if I was a voodoo doll being stabbed by hot needles.

With debris flying all around and bullets ricocheting off every surface, and while enemy fighters continued to fire indiscriminately, I struggled to piece everything together.

I was now very aware that we were caught in a big gunfight but there were many questions that remained unanswered.

Where did they come from?

Why hadn't I seen them before they opened fire?

Why hadn't the surveillance aircraft above us reported movement on the roof?

How many enemy fighters were there?

Where was the rest of my team? Were they OK and the other teams safe?

Our NVGs helped us see well, even in the darkest of nights, but white light, or in this case bright explosions and tracer fire at very close range, blinded us all, adding to the chaos.

While many colleagues have experienced similar confusion in their first significant combat interactions with enemy fighters, it didn't make it any less frustrating that I didn't yet have the experience or muscle memory to make faster decisions or see the full picture in those first moments. That still bothers me.

As the enemy continued to hit us with sustained bursts of automatic fire, we were far from safe. But, rather than looking for answers to the questions fizzing inside my head, all I knew was that we needed to get out of the killing zone as quickly as possible and neutralise the threat the insurgents still posed, or we would all pay a heavy price. This was not a time for rumination, but a time for action.

As I staggered unsteadily to my feet, I found myself with Paul and Chris, who'd both been just in front of me when we made entry. Now a team of three, we would attempt to fight our way out of the enemy ambush and find cover a few houses further down the street, to the left of the target compound. From there we could regroup.

Although we didn't discuss it, I assumed that Ed and Mike had already moved as a pair, having both been on my right, and that they had extracted themselves in the opposite direction. Either way, they had seemingly both vanished.

Paul, Chris and I began our fire and manoeuvre drills, just as we'd practised thousands of times in our infantry training; a procedure that enables team members to move while the others cover them with sustained fire. We hoped that this would give the enemy cause to keep their heads down and take cover for long enough to enable us to get to better protected positions.

I shouted to the others to move first, as I had a good view of the roof and felt well placed to provide the initial covering fire. Emptying almost an entire magazine of aimed shots into the area of the parapet, behind which the insurgents were now hiding, Paul and Chris could begin their extraction down the street.

Once they'd found relative cover, maybe 30 feet or so to my left, they too began firing, with one of them shouting at me to take my turn. I needed no further encouragement.

By this time, one of our own vehicle-mounted machine guns had also begun to lay down a significant weight of fire onto the area of the roof, which was very welcome.

Although in some pain and aware now that I was bleeding, I still hadn't realised that, of the three bullets that had hit or grazed me, one had impacted around half an inch above my left knee, and another was embedded in my right thigh. The upshot of this was that my left leg ignored all instructions to work – the one thing I really needed it to do during the extraction.

This was not ideal.

Each time I tried to put weight on it I fell flat on my face.

As the tactical commander, I was carrying several radios to enable me to communicate with the supporting aircraft flying above, other coalition ground units, as well as with my own team. This weight was in addition to the body armour and other equipment we wore as standard. The upshot was that once I'd fallen, without being able to use both legs, I struggled to get up, instead flailing around like an upturned tortoise.

I felt the panic rising.

Acutely aware that I needed to stop faffing about and get into cover, the more I willed my leg to work, the less it seemed to cooperate, leaving me and my team dangerously exposed. With bullets continuing to buzz all around, the situation remained chaotic.

After falling on my face for the second time, still within the killing zone, I heard someone shout into the radio, 'Zero Alpha is down! Zero Alpha is down!': in military parlance, this meant that I'd been killed or seriously wounded. Yes, I was down, but I was not out, and I remember thinking when I heard it, 'Hang on, I've just fallen over!', slightly worried that, in the heat of the ambush, if they thought I was dead then I might be momentarily left behind.

Although I was still very much alive, I can only imagine what it must have looked like to see me drop like a stone, covered in blood, with the firefight still raging and angry bees looking for targets.

Feeling more than a little anxious, aware that this was not a great place to be left for dead and spitting dust and sand from my mouth, I managed to communicate loud enough over the machine-gun fire to confirm that I was alive and shouted at one of them to 'Please come and pick me up!'.

To my relief, help arrived quickly and, with Chris providing a shoulder to lean on as well as some choice words related to my 'idleness', we managed to hobble away from the immediate danger.

Once out of the killing zone, we made it to the empty plot a few houses further down the street, where there was a degree of protection, affording us a moment to take a breather and regroup. At this point the extent of all our injuries became a little clearer.

Chris had blood dripping from under the front of his helmet, where a good-sized piece of shrapnel had struck him in the centre of his forehead, but without penetrating too deep, thankfully. Only once back at our base did he realise that the chest plate of his body armour had also deflected a direct hit and, incredibly, another bullet had passed under his armpit between his chest and his bicep, scorching a perfect, circular hole in his shirt but leaving him otherwise unscathed.

Paul had also been hit in the face, as well as taking some metalwork in his arm.

In my case, while I knew something was wrong with my legs, in the dark I didn't know specifically why my left leg had been so uncooperative and given way. It was only once we turned on a small torch that I saw the tears in my trousers, where the bullets and shrapnel had passed through and from which blood was leaking down my legs and onto my tan-coloured desert boots.

On closer inspection, we confirmed that one bullet had hit my left knee just above the joint. Entering at the base of the vastus lateralis muscle on the outside of my thigh, it had travelled a short distance internally above my patella, damaging my quadriceps tendon before lodging in the vastus medialis muscle. This explained why it had been difficult to run without falling over.

I was less aware of the bullet that had entered my right inner thigh, but this wound appeared to be several inches deep and, given the fact that the bleeding was slow and steady, we figured it must have missed vital bones and arteries – phew! A much lower priority.

As another colleague, Steve, and his team arrived, he helped me strap a first field dressing to my left knee to stem the bleeding. It was a relief to see that there were no exit wounds, suggesting that both bullets were probably ricochets, thus losing much of their velocity before impact and therefore reducing the extent of the physical trauma. Although the most obvious wounds were the holes in my legs – the source of the dull ache making me feel nauseous – I was now increasingly aware of the smaller pieces of shrapnel beginning to hurt.

The most acute pain, however, was coming from my left buttock, but as it was out of my sight and hurting more than anything else, I was concerned that whatever was going on there could be the more serious wound. I asked Steve if he could 'Please check my arse!' – something I am still teased about to this day. Although he confirmed that there were no obvious wounds, it continued to sting like hell. Only after examination by nurses a few hours later did the source of my discomfort become clear: I had been grazed by a third tracer bullet, whose phosphorous tail had damaged several layers of skin as it whistled by. Despite the burning sensation, I was extremely lucky to have got away with something so minor.

At this point, either through loss of blood or going into shock, or both, I began to feel quite faint. I remember saying to Steve, 'You've got to keep me awake', a phrase I repeated ad nauseam.

Looking back on my career, I think this was the most scared I ever got.

I was not worried about the fact we were still taking incoming harassing fire. I was instead plagued by a niggling worry that, due to the blood I'd lost (conspicuous in the expanding deep crimson stains on my clothing), if I were to pass out, I might not regain consciousness. Even though I later realised that my situation was far from life-threatening, it was the first time I had experienced anything like this. There was a lot to take in, not only medically, but also because I was the team commander with wider responsibilities.

As the heavier vehicle-mounted weapons from our teammates continued to pound the compound, we began to piece together who had seen what and tried to account for the rest of the team.

One colleague reported that Ed, who'd been just in front of me when we made entry, had fallen hard inside the compound as the firing began: status currently unknown. Mike, who'd been just behind me, was still nowhere to be seen, with none of us having any positive news about what might have happened to him after the firing began.

I have no idea how long this regrouping phase lasted, but we were brought back down to earth with a bump when further bursts of automatic fire kicked up dirt near to where we were hunkered down; far too close for comfort.

As the team once again took cover, I screamed in the general direction of the enemy fire, 'For f**k's sake, come on, time out!'. Rather than respecting my request – how rude! – the enemy, who had leapt from roof to roof to follow us down the street and continue their assault, kept firing, forcing us to move again. By this stage, some of the additional adrenaline was wearing off and the stiffness in my legs meant that I struggled to pick myself up off the ground.

It was around then that one of my radios sprang to life.

The supporting aircraft were offering to strafe building 22, where the initial ambush had taken place. Both stated that they had 'eyes on' armed men moving around on the roof, as well as in the adjacent compounds. But when I asked the pilots to confirm exactly which buildings and locations they were referring to, it became clear that they were unaware we still had our own 'friendly' forces in the area, so allowing them to engage risked harming our own people.

Typically, as soon as I tried to pass the message that they were authorised *only* to monitor and *not* cleared to fire, unless given express permission to do so, interference on the designated frequency prevented me from receiving acknowledgement that they had received and understood my message. Although we really needed to move into a safer location, we couldn't do so until we were sure the message had made it through. As the aircraft conducted dummy strafing runs over our heads, my order finally broke through the static and both sets of aircraft gave positive confirmation that they would hold off until actively called in to fire.

Unbeknown to us at the time, Ed, who we were still trying to locate, was far from dead. After taking shrapnel from one of the RPGs, he'd managed to get himself to the back right corner of the compound and set himself up for a big last stand. Deciding that it would be too risky to try and exit through the main gate, where the firing had been fiercest, he calmly built himself a makeshift sangar out of bricks and lined up his remaining magazines and grenades. He made the decision that he wasn't going down without a fight.

My group had been unaware of the enemy's attempts to jump between buildings and follow us to the empty plot, but Ed had a perfect view and was able to stop several of them from successfully making the leap, which no doubt helped prevent us from being overwhelmed by a greater weight of fire when they finally caught up with us further down the street.

Although I had been unable to raise Ed on our team radio, he'd managed to signal to other teammates in the compound next door that, although wounded, he was able to hold his own until an opportunity presented itself to make a break for it.

However, colleagues from the neighbouring team were not willing to wait and a couple of them decided to conduct an audacious rescue before Ed's situation deteriorated. With complete disregard for their own safety, John and Simon rushed the compound to extract Ed.

Having made it in unscathed, somewhat unexpectedly, their return journey was far from guaranteed. Rather reinforcing this point, as each of them made their way out of the compound they were trailed by hundreds more 'bees'. How they avoided getting stung, I have no idea. Luck certainly played a part but Ed, John and Simon's brazen courage and refusal to allow the enemy to call the shots was almost certainly the deciding factor.

The enemy had not foreseen how well-trained, professional soldiers behave when fighting with and for their mates.

While the rescue was in full swing, I was in conversation with my headquarters' leadership. I accepted, grudgingly, that I, and the other wounded members of my immediate team, ought really to be extracted to receive medical care, before our injuries risked putting others in danger.

Yet, I remained anxious that the risk of friendly fire, from well-meaning but not fully situationally aware fire support assets, had the potential to go wrong, and very quickly. As I was the only Brit carrying the necessary radios to communicate with both coalition ground and airborne assets, I wanted to remain on the ground until I could be certain that I was handing over leadership of the tactical battle, with all critical information having been shared and understood with the coalition soldier tasked with overall fire control.

At that moment, an armoured personnel carrier screeched to a halt in front of us, temporarily deafening us, as its large metal tank tracks skidded, throwing up more loose dirt. The thick, armour-plated rear door opened like a drawbridge, hydraulic pumps squealing, revealing a dimly lit interior. In the shadows, I caught a glimpse of several pairs of eyes staring out as Paul and I were bundled in the back for the short drive to an area near the original target compound.

Although Chris had sustained several shrapnel wounds, they were not deemed serious enough to require emergency treatment, meaning that he could stay. Happy to know he was able to fight on, Paul and I were still more than a little frustrated that our injuries didn't allow the same. However, the Sergeant Major was not in the mood for negotiating.

I have always hated being stuck inside armoured vehicles – particularly those without windows – as you lose situational awareness and can very quickly become disorientated. Already feeling nauseous and light-headed from blood loss, the jerky movement as the tracked vehicle spun and twisted its way to the extraction point was an unpleasant experience, flinging us around like balls in a pinball machine.

When the vehicle's main machine gun began firing bursts from just above our heads at targets we couldn't see from below, it made an already disorientating journey even worse.

I don't know what route we took to get to the helicopter landing site (HLS), but we must have been close to the enemy, given the distinctive 'ting ting' of bullets bouncing off the vehicle's armoured plates, on which we were leaning.

The patch of open ground about 75 yards from the front of

compound 22 was designated as the emergency HLS for the medical evacuation helicopter.

On arrival, we were delighted to leave the oven that the rear troop compartment had become. Moving with some difficulty, I hobbled with Paul to a cluster of vehicles now firing long lines of tracer at anything and everything they considered probable enemy movement.

Although it was hard to make sense over the din of the machine-gun fire, I located my equivalent coalition commander, to make sure he was happy with the current situation, including my concerns about friendly fire and the broad intent to neutralise all remaining threats, including clearance of the main ambush compound.

Now confident that all friendly assets had retreated to a safe distance, we gave authorisation for the supporting aircraft overhead to do a few 'gun runs' to neutralise the threat from all remaining insurgents still firing from or hiding on the roof.

At that moment, Ed appeared from the back of another vehicle.

It was only then that we began to learn of his adventures and his expectation that he was going to have to fight to his last bullet. With Ed's reappearance, we had now accounted for my team, but we were still unsure what had happened to Mike, who'd been temporarily attached to our team for this operation.

Ed then relayed the news that we'd all been dreading. He had not made it. Tragically, Mike, who'd been standing so close to me when the firefight began, had been hit fatally.

It's hard to put into words the thoughts and feelings at that moment, but hearing this news opened a complex wave of emotions. Not only did it reinforce how lucky I and my teammates had been to make it through with only a few bullet and shrapnel wounds, but I was also overcome with the realisation that, as the team commander, I had failed to keep everyone safe and bring them all home.

Sadly, it would not be the last time I would experience this in my military career.

Bearing witness to these thought processes in similar situations, be they relief, regret, grief or gratitude, enabled me not to be hijacked by any of them for too long. I've never denied the emotion; what I seek consciously to do is watch it and make room for it until it passes. The first step in being able to do this is the ability to recognise a thought when it comes. In neuropsychological terms this is called 'metacognition'. In other fields it can be called self-awareness, mindfulness or cognitive agility. Whatever we want to call it, being able to do this, whether in the moment or after we are out of immediate danger, gives us a bit of breathing space to manage the ups and downs of our mental life.

During the transit with Paul to the HLS, I had initially felt a wave of euphoria, leading to a brief fit of giggles as we both struggled to comprehend how we'd survived such an intense ambush, particularly at such close range. But this initial sense of relief evaporated the moment the realisation that Mike hadn't made it began to sink in. Any feelings of joy were replaced immediately by a sickening sense of loss and failure.

I began to replay what had happened over and over in my head, trying desperately to picture the situation just before the first bees stung us, when Mike must have been hit. I wanted to find clarity and to make sense of my own actions during those critical initial seconds of the ambush and immediately after I was shot.

I needed to know what I'd missed. What could I have done differently that might have led to a more positive outcome? But it was still all too confusing to make any sense.

The overwhelming need to collate facts and ascertain my sense of responsibility within this and other traumatic incidents is part of the brain's natural response. This is particularly the case, when invested in the situation, when one is in a position of responsibility and accountability. For professionals such as soldiers or first responders, this is important to do. Yet, for anyone, it needs to be approached with caution. There will inevitably be times where one can neither ascertain a logical reason why events unfolded the way they did nor attribute accurate responsibility for it. Right now, I was unlikely to find the answers I was seeking. I needed to move on.

It was at this point that the medical evacuation or medevac chopper, almost unbelievably, began its final approach, while the battle still raged. Touching down, we were once again enveloped in a filthy dust cloud, as well as being bombarded with loose stones, battering our exposed and already damaged skin.

With the helicopter on the ground, we had to move quickly, as it was now extremely vulnerable to enemy fire; a scalp the enemy would dearly love to claim. After a rapid handover of my radios, Ed, Paul and I were loaded into the back for the relatively short flight to hospital.

Being a former army helicopter pilot, I know all too well how challenging flying at night can be, even under normal conditions. But, to do so on operations, relying solely on NVGs, while under enemy fire, is another level altogether.

In our case, these medevac pilots were not responsible for the actions that led to our injuries being sustained, but they played a critical part in the solution. It would have been obvious to them that they would be landing on a hot HLS but they still chose to do so, putting our needs well ahead of their own. Recognising when others step up for us, when they show resilience for our own benefit, is something that not everyone has a chance to experience nor express. Yet, even in everyday life, there may be far more opportunities than we think to take a second to recognise someone quietly putting us first, all of which can be helpful in putting our own challenges into perspective.

After a few very uncomfortable minutes on the ground, and with the helicopter's side door barely shut, we finally leapt into the air, desperate to find safety in the inky blackness of the night sky. How one of the many bursts of automatic fire failed to hit us remains a mystery, given how close we were to the enemy stronghold, but we were all grateful to get airborne without further incident.

Although the inside of a helicopter is extremely noisy, being in the back of this one after all we had just been through provided us with relative sanctuary and calm.

The flight was surreal.

We were all classified as 'walking wounded', even though Ed had ceased being able to walk without considerable difficulty and my own attempts had not been entirely successful. That said, we were all conscious and able to communicate.

I was so grateful, as were they, to be alive, particularly given the devastating news about Mike.

It struck me again how much luck is involved in those crazy moments when all hell breaks loose.

The element that chance plays in life often goes overlooked when we are conditioned to make sense of events and take responsibility for them. Yet, especially in extremely unpredictable circumstances, like so many military operations, given there are so many variables that can influence an outcome, it would be illogical to refute that happenstance is a major player among them.

I felt immense pride at how bravely Ed, Paul, Chris, John, Simon and the wider team had all fought, and I could not have wished for a better bunch of guys with whom to face such challenges.

And, as Ed, Paul and I looked into each other's eyes, sharing relief, pain and sadness, we took each other's hands and retreated into our own thoughts.

Although there was no doctor on board for the flight, paramedics came to each of us in turn, to provide preliminary triage and treatment prior to arrival at the emergency room.

As the paramedic attached a laminated injury card to my shirt I saw that he had scrawled in black Sharpie marker pen 'GSW [gunshot wound] no exit' by each leg, with arrows indicating approximate entry points. As I tried to decipher other codes scribbled on the card, his colleague offered me morphine to ease the pain. I refused initially, not because I was trying to be brave or pretend my injuries didn't hurt (because they did) but because I had the voice of my dear friend 'Spud' ringing in my ears. She had given birth, with some drama, to twins only a few weeks before, without any pain relief other than two paracetamol. So, perhaps fuelled by adrenaline or, rather, stupidity, I had the (what now seems a rather ridiculous) idea that there was absolutely no justification for my taking morphine, as her experience of childbirth sounded far more challenging at that moment than my current issues. It seemed important at the time to demonstrate grit and determination (to myself, rather than anyone else) as a kind of analgesia, although in hindsight, I can see that this wasn't exactly logical.

As I fought to stop the medic inserting the intravenous line in my arm, I tried to explain to him Spud's recent birthing experience and to share my logic. It was clear, however, from his incredulous expression that he neither understood what I was going on about nor had the patience or inclination to battle me over it, so he left me alone for the remainder of the flight.

Drifting in and out of sleep, the orange glow beginning to light up our faces indicated that we were approaching the city. As we descended towards the field hospital's HLS, I could see that there was a medical team waiting to receive us.

Following a verbal medical handover by the paramedics and hospital staff, we were loaded rather precariously onto the back of a quad bike for the short ride to the emergency department.

Once inside, we were relieved not to be split up.

I certainly felt the need to be close to Ed and Paul, after what we had all just been through. Although we were all in the same room, separate trauma teams worked independently to triage and treat each of our wounds.

What was left of my bloodied, ripped trousers were cut off to enable a full examination of my legs. The quartermaster was going to be irritated, of that I had little doubt. As expected, the doctor confirmed gunshot wounds both to my left knee and right inner thigh. From their placement and angle, we surmised that both must have been sustained in the initial burst of fire, when I had been standing, weapon raised, left leg forward. As if I needed reminding, the doctor commented that if the bullet in my left knee had impacted just a fraction lower, it would have likely severely or catastrophically damaged my knee joint, rendering him with few options other than amputation. Eek.

The nurses then cleaned the numerous grenade shrapnel cuts on my arms and legs, while the doctor made notes and decided what operations, if any, he wanted to proceed with, and which could wait until I got home. He determined that the simpler of the two was the removal of metal lodged in my right thigh, as there appeared to be no obvious damage to bone or artery.

What remained of the bullet lodged in my left quadriceps, the doctor recommended leaving to a more specialist orthopaedic surgeon in the UK, as he already had a list of more serious operations to attend to before the end of his shift.

A different nurse hooked me up to several bags of saline via the IV cannula in my arm and, only once I began to feel decidedly woozy did I realise that she'd also added morphine. If this was to shut me up and give them some peace from the constant abuse that Ed, Paul and I were giving each other, I couldn't blame her.

The distance from the trauma triage area to the operating theatre was short and, what seemed like only a few minutes after I was wheeled in under the bright lights, the doctor informed me that he was done, having dug out a decent chunk of twisted metal buried several inches deep. He also took the opportunity to extract several smaller pieces of grenade shrapnel, close to the surface or sticking out of my skin.

Once out of surgery, we were each presented with a specimen jar containing the pieces of shrapnel. Seeing these (now clean and shiny) bullet and grenade fragments rattling around in a sterile plastic container, it felt bizarre to think that only a matter of hours earlier, these had been fired by insurgents intent on killing us.

By the time my team had been discharged, the rest of the group had rolled into our base after a long transit home. After we'd left the battle, they had meticulously cleared the compound, gathering valuable information.

The mood was understandably subdued, but after a 'hot wash-up' of key actions on the target, we gathered in the dining room to toast our fallen comrade Mike. Then we slept.

The following morning, I checked the rest of the equipment I'd been wearing. Only then did I realise how incredibly lucky we had been. Two more bullets had ripped through and torn the fabric of my backpack, just a few inches behind my head, melting the zipper as they passed. Other rips and tears from grenade fragments peppered the rest of the bag; the toll on our team could have been even worse. To have come so close to death, without doubt, changed me and my outlook on life, although it would take some time for the significance of this incident to sink in.

In the days that followed, as Ed and I waited for news about our repatriation to the UK for follow-on surgery, I had a lot of time to think. Given how well the initial operation had gone, I played over in my mind why and how our plan ultimately took such a spectacular turn for the worse.

Once repatriation was the agreed course of action, there was a flurry of activity to ensure we would be given space on the aeromedical repatriation flight back to the UK. Ed and I were both reluctant to leave and tried to convince everyone that, if we stayed, we could still be useful, but the decision had been made and it was the right one. We should go home, regain our health and return to the fight as soon as practicable.

With our departure date looming, it was a difficult time; something I know others felt, too. I continued to analyse what I had or hadn't done and was frustrated that it had taken me precious seconds to comprehend what was going on after the ambush was sprung. I was not yet a hardened combat leader, not yet able to roll with the punches and adapt as deftly as I needed to when faced with complex, dynamic situations. The overwhelming feeling that I had failed as a leader when it counted most hit me hard.

Despite having friends and colleagues around me, never, since my childhood, had I felt so alone. And I didn't feel particularly resilient either.

Losing friends and colleagues in combat is, psychologically, a hugely traumatic event for those who witness it, and a tragedy for the families and friends left behind. And, while our training always drummed into us that we should be ready to deal with death and injury, it did nothing to alleviate the raw pain and emotion when it actually happened, particularly for the first time.

Although I considered myself to be relatively resilient up to that point, this experience and others like it would require me to build and draw on a whole new level of skills to get me and my team through it.

Despite periods of deep reflection and sadness, they were interspersed with waves of positivity and hope.

This tragedy gave us all an opportunity to focus on the things we *did* have, as much as on what and who we had lost. I, for one, recognised that luck had played a huge part in the outcome and, as such, I am fortunate not to have suffered unduly from 'survivor's guilt'. Once Paul, Ed, Chris and I analysed how close each of us came to sustaining considerably more catastrophic injuries, given the proximity of our wounds to vital organs, we thanked God that all of us managed to walk, or hobble, out of danger, even if we had collectively used up a considerable number of our nine lives.

What I failed to acknowledge or think much about until many years later was the impact that this battle and aftermath had on other members of the wider team, as it was not something we ever really discussed.

Only some 15 years after that action did another colleague confide in me how what he had seen that night had deeply affected him. He had been in the compound next door when the firing started and, as he poked his head briefly over the dividing wall between the two properties, he had a brief glimpse of the courtyard where we were fighting for our lives. Whereas I describe the moment the enemy opened fire as being attacked by a swarm of angry bees, he provides a different, but no less chilling, perspective.

As he watched tracer rounds bouncing off every surface, in a kaleidoscope of red and orange, he said it looked as if our team was caught in the middle of a washing machine spin cycle.

After several bullets winged dangerously close to him as well, he ducked back down. What hit him after witnessing the scene was a feeling of helplessness – an inability to change the outcome – combined with a deep sense of foreboding that nobody was likely to survive such a ferocious attack in that confined space, just a few feet away from him.

Consciously acknowledging how others see an incident can be helpful. It takes us out from having an 'egocentric' view, which can feel personal and all-consuming, to seeing others' views from their perspective ('allocentric' processing), from which we can gain objectivity; making room for a sense that we did not experience adversity in isolation and that we are not alone in our response to it (a topic we will cover more in Chapter 6, 'Relationship Breakdowns').

In the years that followed, I read numerous accounts of serious trauma, written specifically by veterans who'd struggled to process what happened to them and others around them.

The more I read, the more a common thread began to appear. Namely, those who were whisked away from the battle to receive life-saving treatment, before they'd had a chance to discuss and process things with their mates, often struggled more. In our case, we were grateful to have a few days together before being split up, but the calm after the storm occasionally gave us too much time to think.

Since becoming an advocate for mental health awareness and support for the military (as well as others who serve their countries and communities in non-military frontline roles), I am now far more aware of the signs of trauma. I am also more aware of the dangers, particularly for those who are exposed, but are unable to get the specialist help they may need or are not able to talk about their experiences. My desire to do more comes, in part, from the fact that after this incident I don't remember being offered any counselling or specialist support, over and above my friends and unit leadership being kind and trying to be empathetic.

I am not saying that anyone was at fault for failing to provide what is now considered non-discretionary trauma risk management support, but the conversation about mental health was almost non-existent at that time. I, therefore, remain extremely grateful that I didn't suffer any long-term mental scars from this or other operational incidents early in my army career, not least as I had little idea where to go or with whom to speak if any one of us *had* been struggling.

Thankfully, towards the end of active service, it became more commonplace for psychological support to be offered as standard, but this was slow in coming.

Through work with amazing charities including the Royal British Legion Industries (RBLI) and Combat Stress, as well as with my wider global military network, I've met thousands of veterans living with the mental and physical scars of their service. But one thing in particular has struck me: trauma does not discriminate. Trauma not only impacts the individual in the heat of battle but can also affect those far from the fight and those we love, many thousands of miles away, making it a very complex and personal issue.

Conscious of protecting my own family during this deployment, I had very deliberately not told any of them exactly where I was going. However, once it was clear that I was going home for medical treatment, I needed to come up with a decent story . . . I duly called my mother to let her know I had been wounded, but she happened to be with my twin sister. The fact that my mother was not alone was not ideal, as it was my siblings who I'd been most keen to protect. So, I warned my mum that I was about to share something potentially a little shocking and asked that she should try and sound as if I had told her something exciting, to avoid freaking my sister out.

I could hear my twin chirping away in the background and made sure that my mum understood what I needed her to do, before explaining that we had been in an incident, that I and my team had been wounded and one of our guys had been killed.

After a brief pause, as she processed what I had said, she responded: 'Oh that's lovely darling, well done!'

I can only imagine what must have been going through her head and I felt bad for asking her to do that, but it did the trick. I went on to explain that I had been shot a couple of times and would be returning to have surgery on my left leg, but she should tell both my sisters only that I was coming home for keyhole surgery for an old knee injury (not entirely untrue). Thankfully, they believed me.

The time for grieving and remembering would come, but this band of determined soldiers had work to do. In the hours and days that followed our Halloween incident, they picked themselves up, processed the situation in their own way and carried on.

Although it was the first of many battles I would survive, this one proved to be a defining moment for me. It had taken many steps to get here but, having been tested, my inexperience as a combat commander was laid bare. In that moment, I recognised the need to learn some valuable lessons, not least that I still had a very long way to go. If I were to become a competent and resilient leader, I must adapt and grow from this experience and hope that next time I found myself in similarly chaotic and confused situations, professionally or personally, I would do better.

I needed also to take maximum advantage of the fact I had got away on this occasion with being only walking wounded and prepare for what was to come.

I wouldn't have to wait long.

PRACTICAL TECHNIQUE: 'YOU GOT THIS!'

In this chapter we have explored how hard it is to find your feet when all around you is in chaos. A very simple technique to cope in such circumstances is to release the reactive tension by exhaling deeply and saying to oneself, 'You got this'. This settles the nervous system and takes the personal sting out of the situation, enabling you to have a sense of trust in yourself to *respond* carefully and not 'react'.

Science and Thinking

Dealing with trauma linked to festivities

*Days of celebration, be they festivities like Christmas or anniversaries or birthdays, can bring with them a sense of frivolity or poignancy, even reflective gratitude. When things go wrong in life on these days and we find ourselves under threat and in harm's way, this can make it very hard for the human brain to compute. RAIN (**R**ecognise, **A**ccept, **I**nvestigate and **N**on-Identify or **N**urture) is a practical 201 Mindful Soldier technique adapted by psychologist Tara Brach. RAIN can help when we **R**ecognise that making sense of suffering on a day of* *celebration is hard,* ***A****ccept the discomfort,* ***I****nvestigate how it feels and gently let it be, taking care to* ***N****urture ourselves (or* ***N****ot to over identify with it as a 'thing' in itself to worry about).*

Safety cues

As mammals, our whole nervous system, our immune system and our emotional regulation systems – the mechanisms that help us to think well, be well and feel well – are inextricably linked to feeling safe: a notion that some even refer to as our evolutionary 'right' (Porges, 2022). Yet, when a sense of threat is pervasive, remembering what safety feels like can elude us. We need to remind our brains and bodies that our first core need is to be safe, and, from that, everything else can flow. This can be done deliberately and is something that police in the UK have been taught since 2019. Practically speaking, we can generate a safety cue by focusing our memory on the moment when we felt in our body the relief of a difficult incident being over. When did we sit back and sigh? How did it feel at that moment? By enriching that memory and keeping it alive, we can neutralise the toxicity of that which was threatening to begin with. Neuroscience suggests that this is best done within an hour of remembering an event (Hanson, 2020).

Episodic memory and time

When we recall periods of acute stress, our brain's depiction of the period's timespan is often skewed by our heightened clarity of some moments over others. As our brains go through this detail, there is a sense that time must have slowed down. Sometimes, there is simply a blur because the circumstances were so fast-moving that the brain was unable to catch up and make sense as it was unfolding, resulting in a lack of detail in hindsight. What is healthy is recognising that sometimes we will remember things in slow-motion detail and other times we won't. When we accept this, we have a better chance to settle with potentially unsettling memories. A practical way to iron out episodic memories like this is to 'timeline' an event to add in more evenly spaced contextual information, so we have a more complete memory to file away as past (Hope et al., 2013; Miller et al., 2020). We can even rewind to what may have been happening before the incident, and then fast forward from the end of the event to the present day, opening up the larger context of what happened and thereby diluting its toxicity.

Watching our thinking (not being a slave to it)

Our ability to monitor our thoughts and learn how to respond to them is one of the most important advances in neuroscience in the history of the human brain (Livingstone, 2003). With this practical skill, we have the capacity to rewire our brain. Sadly, many people miss out on this adventure because they are put off by overuse of the clichéd rhetoric of 'mindfulness' in the early 2010s (Miller, 2022). Whatever we call it, without this skill we are simply at the mercy of an incredibly powerful organ, and the unhealthy 'Default Mode Network' (Liu et al., 2023) thinking it can lapse into, in which we develop dull habits of thought, such as narrating our own day, planning what we want to do next, comparing ourselves to others – all thought patterns that are known to lead to both anxiety and depression. Switching from thinking in the frame of threat perception to that of executive function redirects the flow of energy to the area of the brain that is most advanced, the prefrontal cortex. To do this, we can use a simple 'noting practice', where we take a few breaths and ask ourselves, what am I thinking about right now? How is this kind of thinking helping me right now?

Is it useful? Is it interesting? If someone I care about was thinking like this – in this exact kind of situation – would I encourage them to think differently? In doing so, we force the brain's energy and attention out of the Default Mode Network, into a zone which offers us objectivity, inspiration and self-compassion, all of which helps us maintain resilience (Miyagi et al., 2020).

2

Child's Play

Experiencing Early Trauma and Coping with Instability

> 'Family is supposed to be our safe haven. Very often, it's the place where we find the deepest heartache.'
>
> Iyanla Vanzant, Spiritual teacher and lawyer

I wouldn't become a father until several years after the Halloween ambush, but I already held strong views about parenting and the importance of family. While my own childhood gave me limited insight into what might constitute a 'normal' family life, in hindsight I believe that the dysfunctional nature of my early years played a part in equipping me with some of the skills needed to cope with the challenges I would encounter later, albeit at some cost. Whether being able to bounce back from the physical trauma of being shot, or just being able to get up every time I was knocked down, I am a product of all these experiences.

Being a witness to or a victim of domestic abuse is both shocking and upsetting for anyone at any age, but for children, yet to develop the necessary cognitive skills to understand or process what they are seeing and hearing is even more confusing. I know, because I was also that child. Unfortunately, it is generally not until much later in life that we, as (resilient) adults, develop the ability to look more objectively at challenges and, with open-mindedness and compassion, begin to put our own experiences in context, an exercise which can be helpful. One such incident, however, where the situation was extremely confusing, constitutes my very first memory.

It was 1976. I was three.

A scorching hot summer's day in our small house in a bucolic village in the south of England.

I was suddenly aware of people rushing around, but I had no idea who they were or why they were there.

'Have either of you seen Portia?' my mother asked. Portia was our gigantic brindle Great Dane, my mother's dog for several years before she met my father. Constant companions, they were inseparable, with Portia routinely riding shotgun in my mother's old MG Midget convertible, head poking up above the windscreen, ears flapping in the breeze. My father did not much like Portia and had made it clear that she would have to go once they were married. So, my mother gave her to him as a wedding present instead. Nice work!

Neither my twin sister nor I could find Portia in the house. I have no idea how long we spent looking but eventually a neighbour called to say they'd found her lying in their garden, panting heavily, seeking respite from the blazing sun. I don't remember the exact sequence of events, but in short Portia was losing a battle with sunstroke and, not long after she was brought back to our house, she slipped away.

While my sister watched our first and only family dog breathe her last, we were blissfully unaware that an ambulance was now parked outside and that more strangers were taking my mother in and out of the house to talk.

Unbeknown to us, Portia's death was just the first start of a crazy day; one of a number that punctuated our childhood. This was also the day my father had decided to overdose, the first of many attempted suicides we were to witness as children.

Although I couldn't understand the long-term impact that episodes such as this might have, we felt them viscerally; each one with its own signature, compounding night after night, year after year, creating a cocktail of emotion that was often overwhelming. The knotted stomach with a splash of adrenaline, followed by an emptiness and fear that the cycle of abuse would never end, longing for an escape.

Unsurprisingly, as such a young child, I hadn't yet developed the necessary emotional coping mechanisms and I now realise that I was struggling. However, even just the recognition (now as an adult) of the impact of negative childhood experiences can be helpful in protecting us from building defensive barriers to past realities. Being a child is very different from being an adult, but severing one's experience as a child from our adult understanding of the world does us no favours.

Living with an alcoholic, manic depressive, as my father was, was unsettling, upsetting and confusing, as we never knew which person we would get at any time. With conditions bombarding me and my siblings with signals that something wasn't right, we each began to exist in a state of hypervigilance as the 'normal' attachments to one of our caregivers became increasingly unstable. One challenge we faced was the fact that our father's anti-depressants gave explicit instructions that he was unable or unwilling to follow: 'STRICTLY NO ALCOHOL'.

As youngsters, we didn't know what each of the pills did – they were just 'Daddy's pills' – but I remember clearly that there was always a cluster of small, brown bottles on the bedside table in whichever room he slept. We were told never to touch them, but we did occasionally sneak in to try and read the labels.

What frustrated me then and still saddens me today is that he never once acknowledged having a problem or took responsibility for his actions. All he ever did was articulate, in no uncertain terms, that we – *his family* – were the cause of all issues, an explanation that made no sense to us, especially at such a tender age.

Despite numerous specialist interventions throughout our childhood, nobody was ever able to convince him to take any of the violent, abusive, drunken incidents or suicide attempts seriously enough to get enduring help, something we would have supported fully, had we been able to influence things. Instead, we rolled with the punches for almost 20 years, until my mother finally built up the courage to leave and a court order was placed on him to stay away from us and our home.

Growing up, my father had shown an interest in and had an aptitude for music and art and had spent much of his youth singing in the school choir. After leaving school, he moved to London where his love of English, combined with a keen intellect, saw him become a successful copywriter for national and international businesses. When work flowed, he was professionally fulfilled and had money to burn. During these periods, he could be extremely generous, but his impulsive nature saw him often make irresponsible financial decisions. While he sought to publicly portray a comfortable middle-class existence, the reality was of a far more precarious financial situation. A Jekyll and Hyde figure; frustratingly for all of us, Hyde dominated.

For him, a textbook narcissist, everything was about power and control.

What developed, therefore, was a complex and confusing dynamic. For every opportunity offered by him there was either an ulterior motive or a hidden cost. And the instability that comes with hypervigilance – walking on eggshells for fear of somehow upsetting or irritating him and triggering a violent incident – was only exacerbated by the insecurity of our financial resources.

We were made to feel either guilty or grateful, with a clear inference that everything could and would be snatched from us without warning, should he so choose. This pressure, combined with a sense that he was more concerned about external appearances, left me with a feeling that we were pawns in a game we could neither understand nor influence.

Consequently, much of our childhood was cyclical. We enjoyed periods of relative calm and happiness, but just as we thought these might become the new normal, they were punctured by bouts of excessive drinking, abuse and drama, quite often linked to my return home during school holidays.

Becoming aware that my mere presence was a trigger resulted in home no longer being a safe, secure space for me. It rapidly became somewhere to avoid. By not being there, my young brain surmised that this would be the best way to protect my mother and siblings, as well as myself, from upsetting verbal or physical outbursts.

Thankfully, we were not routinely exposed to violence, but the threat was always there. However, the lack of routine physical violence was more than made up for with emotional and verbal abuse and coercive control, which meant that there was an enduring atmosphere of tension and apprehension.

Even during happier periods, we knew it was only a matter of time before something would trigger a sudden change. I would often count the days in a mental calendar until the next episode.

Life was so unpredictable, making it hard to be a child without facing adult issues that we were neither mature enough nor equipped to process. My sisters and I were trying to navigate adult terrain without knowing the topography, never mind having a map.

We were routinely summoned from our beds late at night.

After returning from the pub, my father would continue to drink excessively and smoke his pipe (any whiff of the brand he smoked still makes me nauseous). Once downstairs, my sister and I were made to sit in our dressing gowns and listen to him berate and admonish us, while he played depressing classical music at full volume; funeral marches were his go to. These sessions could last many hours. As he listed in great detail the things we did that caused him disappointment, we learned, early on, that this was essentially a waiting game. We spoke as little as possible, to reduce the risk of him becoming angrier or, should we answer incorrectly, give him cause to head off on a new and potentially lengthy tangent.

Eventually, he would run out of steam and, once he'd collapsed, comatose in his chair, we would attempt to creep out of the room and head back to bed. Where our mother was for most of these events I don't remember exactly, but it often felt that we were facing many of these experiences alone, not because she didn't want to be there for us, but because she was banished. We had to grow up.

Sometimes, frustratingly, he kept going until the morning, which was exhausting, but when he did finally go to bed, we knew that this would bring us a period of relative calm, as we would often not see him for several days. When he did resurface, he always behaved as if nothing had happened, regardless of what had been said or done. Resentment is too strong a word to describe the way

I feel now, but I am still sad that most my childhood memories relate to similar incidents, all involving my father, none of which were ever followed by any recognition of the trauma and abuse he put us all through.

In hindsight, that was one of the hardest things for us to reconcile; the fact that he never acknowledged, let alone apologised for upsetting or terrorising us. Equally frustrating was the fact that, to everyone else, he was just the jovial eccentric who had a plethora of entertaining stories. To them, he was the life and soul of the party incarnate. None of them saw the darker, more destructive person behind the mask.

What is clear now is that every incident affected me in some way and coloured my behaviour, as well as my expectations, causing me to be labelled often as a difficult child. I was building resilience, but it was not a comfortable process and the manifestation of that was not always constructive.

Even though most of the abuse was verbal, these emotional attacks had equal power to wound.

Threats routinely included giving away or selling our toys or refusing to pay our school fees, but rather than these being inferred, they were explicit: 'When I stop paying, you will be thrown out and never see your friends again.'

However illogical or unrealistic these threats might be to an adult, they were very real for our young minds and led to tears and sleepless nights for most of our early school years.

Unfortunately, there were occasions when my father also revealed a physically violent side. During one particularly shocking incident, my twin and I (we were five or six) were woken by our mother's screams. Sneaking out of our bedroom and peering down into the kitchen through the bannisters on the landing, we witnessed our father grabbing her aggressively by the wrists. As we had been asleep, we had no idea what had triggered this altercation, but it was obvious he'd been drinking.

After watching him spit insults at her for several minutes, with the volume and vitriol increasing with every word, he spun her around suddenly and slammed her into the cabinet by the kitchen sink. Threatening to break her arm, he twisted it violently up behind her back, causing her to scream out again. She begged him to let go, but he was not listening. Seeing this unfold, we pleaded desperately for him to stop and not to hurt her, with tears streaming down our faces. Although in pain, she shouted for us to go back to bed and tried to calm us down by telling us she was OK. Terrified, we retreated to our room, huddling together on our bunk bed, sobbing until she was able to finally escape once he'd passed out in a drunken stupor. Thankfully, she suffered only a wrenched shoulder and some bruising on this occasion, but the incident showed us that he had the capacity for physical violence; a jarring realisation.

I had already incurred his wrath on several occasions due to my 'spirited' behaviour, which had led to me being beaten with slippers and rulers, but the assault on my mother had taken things to another level.

I can't say categorically that it was the psychological impact of this specific event that triggered my response, but I had an overwhelming desire to be able to learn the skills that might enable me to protect everyone – something I had singularly failed to do – should something similar ever happen again. While I didn't think in these terms then, I've since learned that this feeling of having failed is to do with 'smart compassion' – a vehement driver for the acquisition of skill and fortitude, rather than a vulnerability – something we will return to in Chapter 5, 'Never Giving Up'. So, as soon as the opportunity arose, I took up judo. I didn't realise, though, how rapidly I would be putting my new-found skills to the test.

Following the birth of my little sister, a decade later, we were now a family of five.

I had just come home for the school holidays and must have been 15 or 16. As so often, my return triggered an episode. Shortly after I arrived, my father announced that he was going to the pub.

We knew what was coming.

After going to bed, we could expect only a short period of fitful sleep, waiting anxiously for his return. In the early hours I woke to hear the distinctive noise of the taxi's diesel engine ticking over noisily outside, a sound I came to dread. This was followed routinely by the jangling of keys, often dropped multiple times, as he tried to unlock the front door.

Shortly afterwards, the slamming of the door was followed by the sound of funeral music filling the house, often causing me to shake uncontrollably. Recalling this now, I recognise how bizarre this all sounds – had I not been a character on set for this scene, no doubt I'd be both amused and intrigued. However, for our young minds, already hypervigilant to any indication of forthcoming threat, this audio assault was an unpleasant yet routine soundtrack to our childhood horror movie.

With a sense of foreboding, my sisters and I sought sanctuary in our mother's room and waited for the inevitable summons. I watched him through a crack in the door stagger to each of our bedrooms in turn, demanding that we go downstairs 'to talk', which really meant 'to listen' and be 'talked at'.

As I stood in the doorway to my mother's bedroom in my pyjamas, with her and my sisters hunkered down inside, I made it clear that none of us would be going anywhere. Instead, I suggested that he should stop drinking, go to bed and leave everyone alone. Although struggling to stand and slurring his words, he made it clear that he was in charge, that he intended to fight and, after he had beaten me, he would teach everyone else a lesson too.

Seconds later, he lunged.

Using a judo technique learned recently at school, I instinctively employed his own momentum to deflect the assault. Losing his balance, he stumbled and fell down the stairs, ending up in a drunken heap on the landing, hitting his head in the process. Rather than knocking any sense into him, he got unsteadily to his feet, swore angrily and disappeared downstairs.

After hearing the pop of another cork, a different funeral march was selected, reverberating around the house.

I had not meant for him to fall, but it served as a useful warning. In other words, I was willing, and able, to stand up to him (at least physically) and protect my family, even though I wished it wasn't even necessary and, deep down, I was far from confident in my ability to do so. My intention had not been to do any harm, but, rather, to protect and defend. Either way, it appeared to work. From that day, never again did he try to beat me or confront me physically, later confiding that he had no idea what 'other skills' I might have up my sleeve; something he was not keen to find out. He did, however, milk the incident for all it was worth.

On this and several other occasions when he cut his head or blackened his eye while drunk, he would tell anyone who'd listen that I had attacked him. But given his reputation for telling tall tales, it didn't matter and I didn't care, as long as he tempered his behaviour.

While some adults might have found my father's eccentricity entertaining, children generally did not.

A relatively short man, replete with a beer belly, bald head, ruddy features and beard, he cut a distinctive but unimposing figure. With a pipe permanently clenched between his teeth, his appearance alone should not have given cause for unease. However, because of his language and the way he behaved, few of our friends (some of whom he frankly terrified) came to play with us at home, leaving us isolated.

A small hole in the dining room carpet was another reminder of the unpredictable nature of home life; this was the result of the negligent discharge of a 0.22 calibre rifle. He'd been reported to the police by neighbours for brandishing a weapon in a threatening manner (I have no idea why or how this even happened), but when the local police officer arrived to investigate, my father refused to put the gun down or to talk.

He had been drinking, again.

Although we were far too young to know what was going on, it was alleged that my father then waved the loaded rifle at the policeman, who was shouting at him from behind the hedge that separated our garden from the road. The absurdity and dysfunction of our family had reached a new low. The police were equally confused by my mother's attitude who, when asked to bring the children out for their safety, shouted that she would not do that as she had just put us to bed; so inured was she by now to his ridiculous behaviour. However, due to the ongoing risk that the policeman felt my father's actions had on his and our safety, he was eventually taken into custody, but not before a shot had been fired, albeit accidentally.

To me (and any sane adult), looking back and seeing the situation in context, it was ridiculous and far from 'normal'. But, as children, who were becoming increasingly accustomed to this kind of extreme behaviour, this *was*, sadly, our normal. To that end, I cannot say with any degree of confidence if or when we even recognised that we could or should be relieved of this kind of oppression.

Despite the shock of this arrest and confiscation of the rifle, no sooner was he released after a weekend in a cell at the local prison, which included a (almost certainly justifiable) beating from other inmates, he began drinking again.

As much as we were fortunate to live in a nice house in the countryside, I would have gladly given up everything in a heartbeat for a more stable and predictable family life; one in which we didn't go to bed without knowing what horrors the night might bring. And, given that the portrayal of our life was one of middle-class comfort, our childhood trauma was being masked by what society defines as having 'needs met'; yet needs are not fiscal or physical in isolation, they are interpersonal and psychological and the risk of them not being met can, for some, cause more neuropsychological vulnerability than any physical or economic hindrance.

Although I bore no lasting physical scars, I am aware of the emotional impact this existence had on all of us.

I didn't talk to anyone about it at the time, and I am not even sure mental health support was a thing in the 1970s and 1980s, but one way my anxieties manifested was through a recurring childhood nightmare; something I only recently remembered after I heard a friend talk about his own childhood trauma during a mental health podcast. Seemingly, I had buried my own nightmare in my subconscious for over 30 years.

In my dream it is summertime.

The location feels familiar, and I sense it is close to our house, but I cannot place it. I am walking near a river, wearing shorts and wellington boots, with trees and bushes overhanging the footpath. I am both the boy in the dream, seeing things unfold through my own eyes, as well as the observer, viewing at a short distance behind and above the action, from where I'm unable to intervene. I am looking up at the leaves and shafts of bright sunlight breaking through the trees. The beginning of the dream always feels bright, but the light is quickly replaced by a sense of foreboding, of being surrounded, the cause of which is not clear. I then find myself running away from something, towards a wooden stile ahead of me which, despite my repeated efforts, I just cannot reach. I don't know what is bearing down on me, but everything feels dark and threatening. This is my only escape route but the faster I try to run towards the stile, the slower I get, held back by unseen forces. Similarly, the louder I scream for help, the more restricted my voice becomes, to the point where I realise desperately that nobody will hear my cries for help as I can only whisper. With a feeling of utter helplessness, the darkness catches up with me. But before I am entirely enveloped, I wake up, sweating, heart racing.

I have never sought to unpack what might have been the root cause of this recurring dream, or what it meant, but the fact that my sisters and I routinely felt so helpless, waiting anxiously for the next episode from which we could not escape, is likely to be a factor, and constitutes what I now believe would fall squarely into the definition of coercive control.

Invariably, when my father threatened suicide, which he regularly did, he would rattle various pill bottles and rant for hours, before falling asleep, having failed to follow through. He would also regularly call his elderly parents to tell them what he planned to do, before hanging up and unplugging the phone, leaving them distressed and unable to find out if he had indeed killed himself or not. Whether he intended for us to be witnesses to this behaviour, I do recall thinking that it was 'really mean', to scare his parents in this way; grandparents who showed us only kindness and love. In those moments, we were invisible, with him taking centre stage, as was his need, so nothing any of us might or could have said would have made any difference.

One evening, after several false starts, he made it clear that 'this was it' and he was really going to do it.

He went through the motions of asking how many paracetamol tablets would be enough to do the job, woke his parents by calling them on the phone and then staggered drunkenly upstairs.

I am not sure how old I was, but I have a vivid memory of huddling together with my mother and twin sister on the sofa downstairs, watching *Jaws* on the little television in the corner of the living room, wondering when we would be able to go back to bed.

After a while, movement in the bedroom above us ceased.

In the eerie silence that followed, my mother and I tiptoed upstairs to see if my father was perhaps, yet again, crying wolf and had just fallen asleep. However, on entering the bedroom, we found him lying on the bed, on his back, motionless, with several empty pill bottles next to him.

This time it did indeed look like he might have made good on his promise.

Despite the knowledge that seeking life-saving help would likely ensure that this life of cyclical abuse would continue, my mother called for an ambulance. As we waited for the paramedics to arrive, I remember thinking lucidly that, if he died it would be better for everyone, including him, such was the toll that so many years of chronically destructive and abusive behaviour had taken on all of us. I'm not proud of the fact that at that moment I wanted him dead, but I could not see any other way for it all to stop.

As the police and paramedics entered the house our faces were, yet again, lit up with blue flashing lights, as more strangers rushed busily around.

After completing their initial medical examination, the female paramedics confirmed that my father was alive, but only just.

Once stabilised, they took him to hospital, where he spent a week in the ICU, in a coma. With his condition being described as 'poorly', we were advised that, even though he was now getting excellent medical care, the fact that he'd taken so many pills meant he'd done potentially catastrophic damage to his liver and might still not make it. But whether any damage was done, no sooner had he woken up and was strong enough to walk, he discharged himself. Much to the chagrin of the health professionals and psychiatric team seeking to help him, there was nothing any of us could do; an all too familiar pattern.

Although I have shared only a few childhood incidents in these pages, you'll have to take my word for the fact that there were hundreds more I could have drawn upon, each with its own flavour. But, if I did have to sum up, my abiding memory from that time is a feeling of hypervigilance; not necessarily for me but for my mother and siblings. I had seen enough to know from a very early age that things could take a dark and occasionally violent turn with little warning, so I needed to remain on guard and alert to that possibility.

I've since learned from my discussions with Jess that the brain needs to understand why there has been an alarm or an affront to the sense of self, but if it doesn't get that context then the vigilance will remain. The brain cannot turn off an alarm without knowing it is safe to do so, something that rarely came until I took myself away from home. Additionally, she explained that occupations which require hypervigilance are often attractive to those who've experienced this kind of trauma (note career choice). Perhaps more worrying, however, was her warning that hypervigilance, threat of isolation and removal of peer support, combined with the lack of understanding and lack of restorative sleep, when developing as a child is a toxic combination for cognitive development. This, coupled with the reality of being thrust into adult conversations and situations at an early age, which happened routinely, meant that much of our childhood innocence was snatched away.

What did routinely keep us all going, however, was humour. Trying to find something funny in even the darkest moments has been something that started then and has continued to this day, professionally and personally. An element of not taking oneself too seriously, of acknowledging how others see you, but without wearing the label and adding in a touch of humour, are all helpful indicators of cognitive resilience. Noting a tiny bit of humour to the edges of an otherwise not-so-lovely memory can be really good for resilience and features prominently in trauma processing intervention and dealing with challenging experiences, of which I have had plenty.

While my childhood experiences of family did not give me much optimism, I looked for the positives. I consciously tried to bank each experience and how it made me feel and promised myself that, should I ever have a family of my own, I would do all I could to protect them and ensure they would never have to go through what we did. Furthermore, I determined never to allow my children to feel as lonely, scared, confused or upset as I had felt for so much of my childhood.

Although I was becoming more resilient, I was wounded and there would continue to be bumps along the way.

PRACTICAL TECHNIQUE: 'FINDING YOUR FEET'

In this chapter we have explored what it is like to be destabilised from a young age, and at the same time suddenly reliant on oneself to find a way through. The first thing we can do is to quite literally find our feet. If we take a second to physically feel the body firmly attached to the ground, the energy of a massive planet rising up through our limbs, grounding us firmly right where we are, we feel rooted, anchored and strong. With this grounding, our approach to what we face is more steady, more considered and we feel more resolve. From this stance we can settle the overactive mind and withstand better the buffeting of what is going on all around us. All it takes is a few moments of visualisation and we can feel very different, without really changing anything.

Science and Thinking

HEAL(ing)

Making a commitment to recognise moments where we've come through, and deliberately spending time to bank them so that we can call on them in the future is a very practical tool for resilience. When we either recall a time when things didn't work out or when we have a similar situation in the future, we can remind ourselves when things went well. A practical tool has been developed by Rick and Forrest Hanson called HEAL which recommends that when we **H***ave a positive experience, we* **E***nrich it with sights, sounds and smells and all the things that made it what it was, then we really soak in the feeling* *into our body, **A**bsorbing it. We can then **L**ink this positive memory to times that were not so good, thereby neutralising their toxicity and any bias of negativity we may have (Hanson and Hanson, 2018).*

Humour

As we mentioned before, humour can be a very practical form of resilience. Humour connects people. As we share an observation about life that is funny, we release bonding and happiness-inducing chemicals. This can be especially important between people who find themselves in very unusual and harsh situations (Perchtold et al., 2019). If we can learn to navigate difficult terrain with an element of humour, this can be a substantial (albeit subtle) resource in the face of adversity (Dusya and Rodriguez-Lopez, 2004). Humour may well be a personal trait, but there's nothing stopping us from getting into the habit of using it more often.

Hypervigilance and feeling unsafe

Sadly, as a youngster the instability of hypervigilance can easily morph into being unable to trust others and tap into much-needed baselines of feeling safe and secure, which let us know we have everything we (really) need to be OK in any given moment. The conditioning of living without security or a sense of being safely resourced may serve many well in later occupations, such as emergency response and the military, but, in terms of the brain, we do need to tap into a sense of being safe in order to function at our best (Duits et al., 2015). There are practical ways in which we can manage hypervigilance and unease. Essentially, we need to learn to discriminate between what is an inappropriate jumpiness and what is a valid acute sense of alertness to threat. This is important for us to be able to regulate our emotional, immune and nervous systems. The STOP technique comes from the school of Acceptance and Commitment Therapy (Ciarrochi and Bailey, 2008) and has a simple premise: **S***top,* **T***ake a breath,* **O***bserve,* **P***roceed; it is an easy way of regrouping, refocusing and resuming when we feel uncomfortably vigilant.*

When feeling safe at work becomes overworking

Feeling safe with the people around us is important for our brains and bodies (Slavich, 2020). The eradication of home as a safe place is not to be underestimated as it can force a child to attempt to seek security in the non-home life, which in later life manifests as work (Harms, 2011). The potential for overworking in adult life may be one side effect of seeking security from another realm other than home and may not reflect adult circumstances, but an inbuilt coping mechanism learned in childhood.

Affluent neglect

Affluent neglect is the neglect experienced by children in wealthy families; it is often emotional and frequently overlooked, masked by socio-economic circumstances (Brandon et al., 2014). It can expose children to parental issues, such as substance abuse, domestic violence and mental illness, as well as other risks, such as relaxed attitudes to drug use and sexual activity (Matar et al., 2023).

Grieving and child abuse

Wanting an abuser to not be around is understandable. However, this makes grief hard. It is not hard to sympathise with anyone wanting the abuse of themselves or others to have a finite end, and yet this is clearly sensitive territory; notably unchartered by academia (Spence, 2016 and Kong et al., 2021). That said, there are many organisations across the world that openly acknowledge the dynamic of pre-grieving for (or anticipating the end of) abusive parents and offer informal advice on how to deal with such feelings. What is more, grief after abuse can be compounded by a sense of a loss of childhood and the grieving of that childhood itself. In cases of abuse, typically a traditional sense of childhood and all that comes with it disappears – the natural formative stages are gone and there is no guidebook out there to help youngsters bring themselves up, even in the most constructive and functional of environments. Perhaps this is why occupations with structure, meaning and hierarchy can be attractive to those who are doing their own parenting from a young age. There is a lot that we can understand about development from psychologists such as Piaget, who were working in the 1970s and 1980s. Since then, much of what has been learned about how humans develop has been understood more in terms of adverse experiences, such as when children have to grow up fast and say goodbye to being a child at a young age (Neimeyer and Stewart, 1996) or when people join military service young (Riggs and Riggs, 2011).

3

Embracing Uncertainty

Facing Demons, Gaining Independence and Growing Up Fast

'When nothing is sure, everything is possible.'

Margaret Drabble, novelist

Having been identified at junior school as having a half-decent singing voice, in the summer of 1981 I tried out for Winchester Cathedral Choir, where I was, at the age of eight, eventually accepted as a choral scholar.

So began a phase of my childhood that would see me travel widely, grow emotionally and physically, as well as learn some important lessons about independence, teamwork and service. And given the unpredictable and volatile nature of home life, I was fortunate (unlike my sisters) to get a break from the constant shenanigans.

With a punishing schedule of daily choir practices and cathedral services, beginning before and continuing after school, choristers had to board fulltime, which was tough for many, given our age. This was felt particularly acutely at Christmas and Easter, when we were required to stay on for weeks after our friends had already gone home at the end of term, which left about 20 kids rattling around a school designed for several hundred, before being allowed home for what remained of the school holidays. Yet, despite being a demanding existence, it was an overwhelmingly positive period. That said, while the choir provided the stability I craved, I also experienced loneliness. Feeling safer and more settled away from my own family left me both sad and confused.

Unlike most of my friends, who looked forward to going home whenever they could, I dreaded it. The fact that the word 'home' did not conjure up feelings of safe rootedness, safety or familiarity was clearly unusual and might seem inexplicable for many. Instead, 'home' for me was somewhere I felt a sense of risk, danger, pain and anxiety, rendering the term meaningless, given that it came with a sense of threat.

So, as the end of each term approached, I became more anxious, conscious that my homecoming would probably cause an incident or episode of some kind. I desperately wanted to spend time with my mother and sisters, but I felt guilty about the effect my return would have on them once attention might not be, for a moment, on my father, which was a regular trigger.

This made life both unsettling and uncertain. I didn't like it.

These pressures, and my inability to process them, certainly contributed to my less than exemplary behaviour, resulting in my fair share of physical beatings at school. Although I can remember only a few of the things I was punished *for*, I vividly recall what I was beaten *with*: these included a cane, hairbrush, ruler, clothes brush, plimsole and even a wooden parquet floor tile from the classroom. I know (it was the 1980s).

However, despite constant angst about family, the most powerful memory from this time was a sense of opportunity: performing to huge audiences, new adventures and the exhilaration of international travel.

Having the chance to sing in some of the most iconic venues around the world was a huge privilege – from concerts with the Vienna Boys' Choir in the Musikverein to New York's Carnegie Hall and the Dorothy Chandler Pavilion in Los Angeles – we experienced it all, as well as appearing regularly in front of live television and radio audiences. Being flown to New York to perform the world première of Andrew Lloyd Webber's *Requiem* was a particular highlight.

As an unworldly 12-year-old, to be whisked away from school for a week, put up in a swanky hotel on Fifth Avenue, given $250 spending money by Lloyd Webber himself (a considerable sum in 1985), and then performing in a live broadcast to more than 60 countries was surreal. Yet, as children – already relatively seasoned performers – we took it all in our stride, unfazed, nerveless, devoid of the self-doubt most of us would later experience. Thankfully, we were enjoying and benefiting from what I understand Buddhist neuropsychology refers to as a 'beginner's mind' – a highly valued, privileged and under-respected position; one in which we are able to see life in its utmost purity and raw reality, without inherited bias, conditioned angst or misplaced compliancy (pollutants we all tend to pick up through life).

Following the success of the world première, we later performed the British equivalent in Westminster Abbey, where Prime Minister Margaret Thatcher was the guest of honour. Very generously, at a Downing Street reception afterwards, she gave a few of us a tour of No. 10 and even replied personally to my precocious handwritten thank-you letter, which I took to mean that we were now BFFs.

We were then asked to record the *Requiem* album in the 'Beatles Studio' at EMI Abbey Road in London, which, as a Beatles fan, was the most amazing experience of my life to that point.

The album proved to be remarkably popular, achieving triple platinum status in only a few weeks, with the single 'Pie Jesu' reaching number three in the UK charts, earning us a slot on *the* music show of the era, *Top of the Pops.* With television requests also coming thick and fast, I found myself singing on various shows, including *TV:AM* (the biggest national morning show at the time), joining the legendary horror film actor Peter Cushing, among others, on the sofa for a chat. All pretty random, but I was learning to seize every opportunity and live in the moment, not least because I had no idea if or when it might all be snatched away.

Although the singing and choir was going well, I was struggling on an emotional level and began a period of self-destructive behaviour that saw me do risky things. I justified them as being 'for fun', but I recognise now that I was probably attention-seeking as I wrestled with my domestic familial challenges over which I had no control.

I began encouraging and accepting stupid dares, which saw me variously jump out of upper-floor classroom windows, climb very tall trees with zero regard for safety and cut my arms with a craft knife to gauge my pain threshold.

I don't remember my thought process, probably because there wasn't one, but I do have a strong sense that I didn't really care if something happened to me. That said, not once did I ever have suicidal thoughts, but the idea of hurting myself didn't worry me either. Perhaps, by dint of the number of episodes and suicide attempts involving my father that I had already witnessed by that age, I had been inured to the idea of death. I'm not sure. Unbeknown to me then, there are models of trauma processing that help explain how an individual who has survived traumatic experiences can sometimes have a slightly altered sense of danger and risk. Perhaps the exploration of my pain threshold was me testing my own tolerance and boundaries as a reference point for future life? Either way, my behaviour was clearly not sensible and suggested that I wasn't coping; not that anyone in authority seemed to be looking.

I wondered, therefore, if the move to my senior school would be the change I needed; a fresh start, further from home, with new opportunities to keep me occupied.

After five long years of dedicating my life to music and singing, I was tired. The last thing I really wanted to do was to commit to more of the same, as I loved sports and art and worried that being labelled solely as a musician would preclude me from engaging in other pursuits. However, as a choral scholar, I was expected to apply for a music scholarship and, given the reality that our family's financial situation was far from secure, we really needed me to win one. The pressure was on.

Due to the cyclical nature of my father's alcoholism and depression, cash came and went. Despite his ability to deliver quality work when focused, he began to lose contracts and clients when he missed key deadlines or failed to deliver at all.

While my singing was strong, I was less confident with the instrumental requirements. As a result, I failed to get a full scholarship. I was instead offered a 'Music Exhibition' for my singing alone, but this still required me to play the flute and piano. This lesser award, combined with doing just enough to pass the entrance exam and finding a housemaster willing to give me a chance, meant I was offered a place. But rather than being excited, I began to panic. Not only was this school by orders of magnitude bigger than my little choir school, I worried that I wouldn't fit in, not having come from money.

As soon as I arrived at my new school I felt completely out of my depth, an imposter. However, until or unless I was found out, I made a conscious decision that I would make each moment count, taking advantage of all the amazing facilities the school had to offer and grasping every opportunity that presented itself. Yet, despite approaching this phase with a positive mental attitude, I experienced my fair share of setbacks and shocks, the first of which came at the end of my first year.

I knew I'd scraped in academically, but I was not prepared for the brutality of the system used to grade students in the annual exams. Regardless of the overall quality of the year group, we were ranked from top to bottom, with names read out publicly in the school theatre, making it abundantly clear to friends and fellow students exactly how you had performed (or not). Long story short, I placed 247th out of 249 students at the end of year one.

I was mortified.

Whether people were looking, pointing or whispering, I don't know, but it felt as if hundreds of eyes were boring into me, judging me. I just wanted the ground to swallow me up. Immediately afterwards, I was summoned by my tutor and remember clearly walking to his house, shellshocked. I didn't know what to say. I just felt nauseous, convinced that I would be asked to leave the school; yet more uncertainty and chaos in my life. Had I just thrown away this incredible once in a lifetime opportunity? To say that my heart was pounding would be an understatement.

While many of us will be familiar with the rush of a near miss or sudden fright, this was different. The common 'startle response', I now understand, is one component of the body and brain's reaction to a signal that something is wrong and needs our attention; the physiological components of which can be an increased heart rate, heightened senses, tension in the muscles or shallow and rapid breathing as the body prepares for action. All these are helpful for dealing with a momentary threat. However, in my case, when these threats are more than one-offs and inextricably linked to places or people where or with whom one should feel safe, the response can become problematic; when the brain and body struggle to keep up it can result in a freeze or dissociation (where you may feel detached from your body or feel as though the world around you is unreal). This is the situation in which I found myself.

In this particular moment, as I approached my tutor's house, where my fate might well be sealed, my stress response was almost unmanageable. Expecting to be categorised a 'General Total Failure' (GTF), reserved routinely for the bottom three students (and yes, it was still the 1980s) I listened in disbelief as he spared me, awarding only two GTFs. However, it left me feeling still very much out of place and with a sense of shame.

Only with many years' experience do I now realise that, while shame may not be that uncommon in contemporary adult education (notably for medical students), it can be really unhelpful and act as an inhibitor of trauma resilience, that is to say, shame can actually exacerbate symptoms of trauma and prevent individuals from accessing help or engaging in support. How we manage shame is key to our resilience.

Desperate not to waste the unexpected second chance I had been given, I needed to switch mentality: from the panic of the startle or fear response, to one of resolve and open mindedness. If I was to have any chance, I needed to reset my acute stress response, allowing more creative decision-making to take over. I was beginning to learn a critical skill for building resilience, namely being able to switch between dealing with the immediate threat, but also seeing the longer game ahead.

With this in mind, I threw myself into as many extracurricular activities as I could: rugby, rowing, cross-country running, music, art and judo (for use in the school holidays, if required . . .), as well as knuckling down in the classroom. Thankfully, this new mindset enabled me to move up the student rankings over the next few years and into a more comfortable position in the top half of the year group, where I managed to stay.

Much of my life, however, continued to spin out of control.

Not only was I dealing with the pressure of being in an environment in which I felt inadequate, I worried constantly about whether I could fix our toxic home life. As a consequence, I was often not a pleasant person to be around; something for which I am ashamed.

Family dramas, combined with overactive teenage hormones saw my emotions see-saw routinely from happy and charming to moody, aggressive and downright difficult. This required deft handling by the teaching staff and some very tolerant and understanding friends to whom I will be eternally grateful for not giving up on me. I should make clear that, despite being able now to look back at those moments and admit that I was far from my 'best self', any objective self-awareness (or self-compassion for that matter) at the time was, shall we say, limited. Only with repeated exposure to challenging circumstances have I learned how to maintain self-awareness in the moment.

Since speaking openly in recent years with friends from school, they said they'd had no idea what I was dealing with and most denied that I was appallingly behaved, but I know I was. What has been most illuminating about those conversations, however, is that some of my friends had, it transpires, equally challenging and abusive childhoods, yet none of us thought to share. I wonder now how things might have been or felt different at the time had we clubbed together, a peer support group of parental abuse survivors.

One thing my school did brilliantly was help every student identify and then explore their particular passion. I relished the opportunity to get deep into art and sport as positive outlets after realising that any concern about being different – financially or otherwise – was not a factor in the studio, on the rugby pitch, river or in the dojo.

Despite committing to my sport, success did not come easily, as I always seemed to be the smallest and had to work hard to justify or keep my place in every team. I did, however, achieve a modicum of success by being selected both for the England Schools' (South) rugby team and the Great Britain junior rowing squad. But this too became a stressful balancing act, routinely requiring me to run from a rugby match's final whistle to the gym, battered, bruised and covered in mud, to join rowing training sessions, thereby proving (or hoping to prove) my equal commitment to each team's coach. A quick hello to my mother, who supported me loyally from the touchline in every rugby match she could attend, and then on to the next thing.

Inevitably, something had to give and, shortly after turning down an invitation to attend England rugby final trials (to focus on rowing), I was unceremoniously dropped from the school 1st VIII.

I was devastated. However, I learned (albeit with hindsight) several valuable lessons. I was angry and disappointed at being deselected, but the fact that I can still look back and remember viscerally the emotions in that moment reinforces how powerful and necessary they were.

Once I'd overcome the overwhelming sense of loss of my team family, being forced to pick myself up and build emotional strength was an important experience; not that I consciously felt I had much choice in the matter at the time. But understanding the importance of self-reliance and developing grit became a key factor, something I would need to hone even further in the years to come.

Failure is not fun. Living with uncertainty is not fun either, but I can assuredly say that I have learned more through my failures than successes. Equally, being forced from an early age to accept and get comfortable with uncertainty and having to adapt and learn, particularly in the face of adversity, has made me far more resilient in navigating life's challenges.

To that end, I now view complexity and uncertainty as a gift; an opportunity to live by the mantra cited at the top of the chapter, 'When nothing is sure, everything is possible.' We just have to open our eyes and our minds to find it.

Yet the punches kept on coming.

With just about everything my father did being about exerting control, and with less than two years to go until I finished school, he stopped paying my school fees. So, when I was called to a meeting in the headmaster's office I feared the worst. Sick with dread at what I thought was to come, I assumed he was going to inform me that I would have to leave. Instead, he told me calmly that he understood what was going on and that he was unwilling to allow my potential to be snuffed out.

Instead, he said I could complete my schooling, regardless of whether my father paid or not, because I was a net contributor to school life, through music, art and sport. To say this was welcome news is an understatement, but I am not sure I really listened to what he was saying. I just wanted to be sick.

I believe that the kindness that both the headmaster and his wife showed saved me from taking a destructive and potentially devastating path. He was well within his rights to kick me out, but the empathy and understanding he demonstrated was genuinely life changing. Decades later, I still mentally reference this meeting and, when I find myself in danger of treating others with less compassion than I should, I try to check myself and think: 'I wonder what Poppy and Eric would say?'

I later came to realise that, while I always assumed that I was an imposter, financially at least, more than a quarter of students received financial grants and support of one form or another: something on which the school quite rightly prides itself. Again, if only I had been aware of that at the time, perhaps I wouldn't have felt so out of place. Despite the school's generosity, however, being allowed to remain came with additional pressure.

Although never spoken, in my own confused mind the message from the headmaster had been clear: 'You can stay because you are contributing to school life . . . but the moment you cease to add value, the deal is off.' And so, this subconscious and entirely self-generated pressure meant that my world remained stressful and unpredictable.

Such was the upsetting nature of returning home that I became increasingly keen to avoid having to go back at all when each term ended. As the day approached, I became more uneasy. I needed to find a way to acknowledge my unease, but not let it consume me to the point that I would be unable to see a way through. I had to find the freedom that exists in the gap between stimulus and response; something Auschwitz survivor Viktor Frankl credits as being the deciding factor in his own survival, despite appalling odds. By teaching ourselves to watch our thoughts before we get hijacked by them, we can, over time and with practice, widen that gap and gain real liberty and empowerment.

But where would I go? Where *could* I go?

I had to get creative.

Being an aspiring artist, I sought out commissions that I could complete quickly – paintings or drawings of people's pets or houses – that might enable me to earn enough money to buy a plane or train ticket and head somewhere independently.

Anywhere but home.

If I was physically absent, I could better ameliorate the risk and avoid exposing my mother or sisters to unnecessary drama, so often a consequence of my return home. Although friends often offered to take me in, I was not good at accepting their hospitality and kindness. I had developed an ability to push people away. I would often lie, saying I had other plans, even when I didn't, to avoid being a burden. Completely illogical, I know.

When I did accept, I tried to learn lessons from the other families I spent time with, whose unconditional kindness showed me that there was indeed another way. One such family was that of my best friend from school, a close-knit Scottish family who lived a simple life in Italy. I will be forever grateful to them for the escapes they offered me when I needed them most; where I was safe and happy. But these incredibly positive periods of love and warmth were also tinged with sadness when reminded that such sanctuary was only temporary.

Thankfully, there were still a handful of other friends too, who also refused to take no for an answer, one of whom prevented me from getting caught up in an extremely serious incident.

On one break from school, my plan had been to sleep rough at Paddington station until school resumed. There was not much more to it than that, but I didn't care. So, when I saw, from the comfort and safety of a friend's house (who had insisted I went home with him to his family instead), news of an overnight terrorist bombing of the station, I threw up. Thankfully, nobody had been hurt or killed, as the station had been empty, but the nature of my situation suddenly became very real.

While there were many negative consequences of an abusive childhood, they sparked a desire to find independence and branch out.

I learned early on that if I wanted to do something, nobody was going to give it to me. If I wanted to travel, I should find a way of making it happen. On my own. But even with this sense of freedom, resilience and independence that I was beginning to enjoy, I was unable to fully embrace it, as the situation at home had now reached breaking point. After my father had taken another serious overdose, with associated threats of violence, social services intervened. Enough was enough.

My father was issued with an injunction ordering him to stay away from the house on pain of arrest. Typically, all this was unfolding as my twin sister and I were preparing to take our final school exams. I remember vividly the telephone conversations I had with each parent around that time, passing messages between them. Playing the intermediary was understandably difficult, particularly if either side reacted badly to the message being passed on. 'Tell her . . . tell him . . .' was the way conversations went, with me performing a role for which I had neither auditioned nor welcomed.

What it did teach me, however, was that using children as a proxy is *not* OK, under any circumstances, and that I would never allow something like this to happen if I ever had children of my own.

Back in my teenage world, such was the emotional turmoil of everything going on, my conduct at school took another unhealthy turn. Sick of being in the middle of adult issues and the uncertainty of what would happen – which I assumed meant the sale of our family home to pay off my father's debts – I just stopped studying. I needed to be a child again; to be given a break from living in the grown-up world of 'adult mode' or 'parent mode'.

I felt angry and, while I wanted help and attention, I didn't care if anybody noticed.

Half of me wanted to fail, just to make a point, but I was conflicted, as I also wanted to prove everyone wrong and show them that I *was* capable and *could* make something of myself. But having been told for years by my father that I would never amount to anything and that I was stupid, my confidence was dented and fragile.

In the end, I got through all my end-of-school exams without significant collateral damage (despite concerted sabotage efforts on my part) and, thankfully, managed to avoid a scenario in which options evaporated due to my lacklustre performance. It was touch and go.

I was living on the edge; decision-making skills compromised.

Two decisions I did get right, however, were to apply to university and to have a gap year before taking up my place; the latter affording me an opportunity to teach history to a class of cheeky eight-year-olds and to accept an invitation to play rugby at Harlequin FC, mixing with and learning from England rugby royalty.

The other significant decision I made was to join the school's combined cadet force (CCF), my first direct encounter with anything remotely military. We were fortunate to have some very experienced instructors – Parachute Regiment veterans – most of whom had seen action in the Falklands in 1982. They took me under their wing and encouraged me to think about a career in uniform, something to that point I had not considered, despite my maternal grandfather having crewed bombers of various types in the Royal Air Force throughout the Second World War.

Although I don't remember the content of the lessons we received, I do remember the feeling of trust and teamwork that having adventures in small teams gave us as we played soldiers for a few hours each week. Even though I certainly didn't see it or realise it then, these were powerful, soul-shaping, career-defining moments. Being exposed to this new world left its mark.

So, while my school years proved to be a mixed bag, with plenty of setbacks, failures and lengthy periods of uncertainty, it was also a period of hope; a hope that things would and could get better. I just had to stick the course.

I didn't want to let the negative experiences hold me back. And, despite the issues I faced (and the many I created myself), I began to realise that I would survive and, if and when knocked down, I could and would get right back up and keep going, more resilient than before, learning all the while that uncertainty was a far more positive and exciting space than I had realised.

PRACTICAL TECHNIQUE: 'DON'T KNOW'

In this chapter we have explored that sense of not knowing what might be ahead of us: our fears, opportunities for freedom or requirement to adapt. We may feel bombarded with potentiality and 'What Ifs'. Sometimes it's the What Ifs that can perturb us more than what is actually happening. Brains can get locked in a battle with hypothetical scenarios that 'may' or 'could have' happened, taking our energy away from the here and now, and adding an unhealthy dose of self-doubt. One of the most simple and pragmatic moves in these situations is to accept *not knowing* everything. Life is full of unknowns, some of them will always remain, and this is something we just have to work with. Try it for yourself, and you may find a real sense of calm, wherein you are more open and where solutions are much more likely to come to you.

Science and Thinking

Taking responsibility for an abuser

When the child of an abuser takes responsibility for the abuser's outbursts and abuse, they see themselves as a prompt for that behaviour, which can bring about a powerful message to the psyche that may not be commonly understood. That message we tell our inner self is that we can cause harm. The weight of this on a child or a teen can be a heavy one, relief from which may only come when it is counterbalanced with a duty to contribute and do good in order to rectify that balance. This may be a powerful driver and motivator for a survivor in later life, but it does beg the question as to whether this is really fair? Is it OK to commit yourself to a life trying to rectify the impact of others' behaviour, or – as the adage goes – 'the sins of the father'? Author Neil Strauss (2016) is known to have refreshed this biblical and Shakespearian saying to: 'The sins of the parents are the destinies of their children. Unless the children wake up and do something about it.' A practical way of preventing oneself from overidentifying with others' wrongs is simply to remind oneself that they are not us, that we are separate from them (Miller, 2022). A simple technique would be to take a breath and say to oneself, 'This is not me, I am not that, this is not mine'. In Buddhist psychology this is known as 'Anatta' or 'not self'.

Dealing with uncertainty and instability

Brains by default do not like lack of safety or stability, nor are they that enamoured of uncertainty. Yet, brains can become used to adapting to those environmental conditions, and in that adaptation (ironically) we find familiarity: something the brain does like. Where we are having to navigate familiar territory, we are efficient in our application of our resources, therefore leaving us with more energy to spend on things that our brains and DNA really, really want us to do, such as eat and procreate. So, dealing with uncertainty is vital for resilience. Getting used to not knowing can be as simple as using a technique formulated by Western Zen expert Jon Kabat-Zinn in 2005: when your mind is buzzing with insecurity and questions, just acknowledge this with the words, 'Don't know'. With practice, this can become very liberating. When we say this, there is no consequence, no weight of expectation, no further questions needed. In that space of calm, ironically, answers are more likely to arise subtly. Similar to this is the notion of 'beginner's mind'. Being able to value those moments of childlike rawness gives us as adults the chance to reclaim a fresh perspective, freer from the baggage we have accumulated over the years. Zen teacher Suzuki states: 'In the beginner's mind, there are many possibilities, but in the expert's, there are few' (Suzuki et al., 1970). Sometimes accepting that we are here to learn on this planet is the smartest move we can make.

The ambiguities of self-harm

Understanding the parameters of and drivers for self-harm is critical in contemporary culture, and it is important to recognise that the physical injury to the body is not necessarily representative of a desire to harm oneself (or of suicide ideation) but to understand and to express, in order to live. The complexities and ambiguities of self-harm are being researched further as it becomes a more common phenomenon in young teens and adults (Simopoulou and Chandler, 2020).

Stress response and repetitive alarm

The human brain adapts and maladapts to the repetitive alarm of threat after threat after threat, be it in one's personal life or professional occupation, and this has consequences for well-being and public safety (Miller, 2022; Boyer et al., 2022). As we mentioned earlier, recognising what is a genuine threat and what is our habitual hypervigilance to things (making us feel inexplicably on edge) is as key to our well-being and happiness as it is for accurate threat perception (Covey et al., 2013). It can be helpful to really take a second to respond to that seemingly inexplicable sense of something not being right by asking oneself what the danger is. This can take a matter of seconds using this practical technique (Miller, 2022): take the words FEAR and THREAT to use as acronyms so we can ask ourselves, what is this? Is it ***F****alse* ***E****vidence* ***A****ppearing* ***R****eal (Fear) or a* ***T****rustworthy* ***H****eightened* ***R****esponse:* ***E****ffective* ***A****nd* ***T****actical (Threat)? If we sense that we are loading the sense of apprehension ourselves, adding a subtle narrative as we perceive it, then this may well be our fear talking. But if our response is more pragmatic and responsive, it may be us better dealing with threat. There is a subtle difference between feeling fear and perceiving threat, and that is appropriateness. We can only manage how appropriate our responses are if we get to know them. We can practise this by taking a moment where we have felt threatened and asking ourselves if the fear was proportionate (sometimes it will have been and sometimes it may not have been). By doing so, we become better evaluators of risk, a quality that those re-exposed to challenging incidents need in order to protect their mental and physical health (Covey et al., 2013).*

The link between shame and resilience

Shame can really get in the way of us moving on from difficult experiences in our personal (Saraiya and Lopez-Castro, 2016) or professional lives (Markman et al., 2019). It can be very quietly paralysing. Sometimes the only practical remedy for this is to roll up one's sleeves and reinvigorate one's resilience using some self-compassion. This does not come easy to those used to giving or protecting and caring about others (either because of our upbringing, family or social situation or our jobs), but it is critical to disarm shame and release effective decision-making. This is often conceptualised with the wording of the oxygen mask instructions in air travel: 'Always fit your own mask first before helping others.' Another way of dealing with shame is to see it as an unnecessary addition to something we have already found difficult. In contemporary Buddhism this is known as 'shooting the second arrow' (Bhikkhu, 2013): when we know we are suffering, we can accept that without adding a reason not to regain our resilience.

Building resilience through sport

Being different at school, worries about whether we are accepted or not by our peers, are no doubt common anxieties across generations of young people. What is more, we know that sport and physical activity can be an equaliser for those feeling different from others for non-visible reasons. (It can also be a massive divider for those not physically able to compete.) Throwing oneself into sports can be a chance for some to temporarily put aside internal worries and ruminations about family circumstances and background. This is something that is being more widely socially accepted as a constructive approach to supporting those with adverse childhood experiences, who may spend so much of their time sensing their difference more than their equanimity with others around them (Norris and Norris, 2021). What is more, some forms of aerobic exercise, such as running, have been shown to stimulate the hippocampal formation in the brain, which we use to contextualise difficult experiences, thus helping the processing of recent trauma and building capacity to do so over time (Inoue et al., 2015; Miller, 2022).

Feeling kindness and compassion

Really feeling the kindness of others is incredibly valuable to resilience. For many who have suffered abuse, trust can be difficult and may often take the shine off others' acts of care. Being able to see compassion in others is now known to really boost mental resilience and is being taught in the context of meditation (Kirschner et al., 2019), encouraging those who are interested in training their brains to use it as a resource. What is more, neuroscience has given us a great deal of insight over the last 20 years. One gem is the brutal reality that the human brain is physically unable to feel fear and compassion at the same time (Miller, 2022). The result of this is that compassion can become a powerful weapon for stress management when we feel ourselves being disproportionately threatened by a situation in which we could do with acting smartly. When we learn to activate low levels of compassion, we can immediately quieten our nervous system and once again stimulate the smartest part of our brains, the prefrontal cortex, to be able to make good decisions. This is called 'smart compassion'. Low levels of compassion could be feeling slight (and ever so slightly smug) pity for someone who's behaviour is atrocious, by acknowledging that although we must deal with their attitude right now, they have to wake up each day and look in the mirror and see that potential for monumentally messing up staring right back at them. A less judgemental approach is to take a moment to consider all the influences on that person's life, how they learned about the world and their current circumstances that pushes them (perhaps even unwillingly) towards this mentality.

Negotiation and communication

Literature on adverse childhood experiences (e.g. Johns et al., 2021) has explored the complexities of how early experiences may both enhance and hinder different types of negotiation in later life, but the message is clear: early life experiences can be fertile ground for life lessons that may equip adults in skills they may have not otherwise had the opportunity to hone.

4

Self-Doubt and the Perception of Failure

Choosing Self-Kindness and Calm over Chaos

'Doubt kills more dreams than failure ever will.'

Suzy Kassem, poet and philosopher

Friends and colleagues often make fun of my inability to sit still or do just one thing. They watch me, often bemused, running around spinning plates as I take on a plethora of personal and professional commitments. While I have always prided myself on having a can-do attitude, one consequence of this is that I am not as good as I should be at saying 'No!'

Believe me when I say that I love the idea of a simpler life; one with fewer moving parts. However, it's a concept I struggle with. I *am* trying though. Genuinely.

The recommendation from a friend to read Greg McKeown's *Essentialism: The Disciplined Pursuit of Less* during one of the six weeks I spent locked in a Sydney hotel room during Covid-19 (in order to secure time with my daughter) has been extremely helpful in reframing for me the concept of meaningful contribution. My implementation of his concepts does, however, remain a work in progress.

So, why do I feel the need always to do more? Pausing to ask myself this question is something I've only focused on since writing this book. Yet taking time every now and again to ask questions about ourselves and our standpoints in life can be an enriching experience. Approaching the exercise with an inquiring mind, open to development and learning, can lead us to insight and ultimately to resilience. It is important to note, however, that if we dwell too long and we find ourselves in a stasis of bewilderment or navel-gazing, this can instead restrict opportunities and diminish our resilience over time.

In my case, a passion for learning and an ongoing search for meaning and purpose are certainly factors in driving my adult behaviours, but I believe it also stems, at least in part, from my school experience. In a sense, I am constantly playing out my final years, acting (albeit subconsciously) as if I risk being kicked out or judged for not contributing or 'adding enough value'.

Taking on multiple endeavours can sometimes be daunting, but it feeds a sense of curiosity and fuels my desire to continue to grow, so I don't necessarily see my approach as a negative one. As with so many things in life, the key is being able to strike a sensible balance. The enjoyment I derive from working with interesting people in interesting places doing interesting things – features of my careers, in and out of uniform – is addictive; in the same way athletes feed off the positive feeling dopamine gives them after strenuous exercise.

Yet, self-doubt often remains. But that's OK, too; it's how we deal with the doubt and explore the opportunities that come from it that makes the difference.

Anything other than overwhelming success does not necessarily constitute failure. However, this is the lens through which I've absolutely viewed life in the past. Within this dominating narrative, I've often failed to consider the role of perspective. What one sees or feels is routinely very different from how others see (or judge) you.

As the philosopher Criss Jami posits in his book *Killosophy*: 'The biggest and only critic lives in your perception of people's perception of you rather than people's perception of you.' With this in mind, we can probably all be kinder to ourselves, although that's easier said than done.

As with any skill, it requires practice.

While I recognised at school that I was never likely to be big enough, strong enough, talented enough or fast enough to compete at the very highest level in any sport, I was determined to try and just see how far I could get, imposter or otherwise. I figured that, even if I was unsuccessful, the experience of having tried would make it worthwhile. I would hopefully learn something valuable, even though failure might be hard to deal with at the time.

On the (many) occasions I've been told I would be unlikely to succeed, it has just made me even more determined (Taurean that I am) to disprove the naysayers and given me an opportunity to demonstrate grit and resilience.

There was a time in my professional life when I had to apply for a staff officer role (a desk job), but when the list was circulated almost all the job descriptions sounded incredibly dull. Only one piqued my interest: working in the Army's Strategy Branch, helping to draft speeches for the Secretary of State, writing British Army strategy and working closely with internationally recognised London-based think tanks. While I was aware this would be a stretch for me, it sounded fascinating. When I asked around, however, I was told that the job had already been offered 'off the books' and would not therefore be open to me or anyone else in a normal selection process. I was incensed and duly submitted my application for that role – and *only* that role – in an arguably truculent attempt to force a fair selection process to be run, as it should be. However, this was far less about me and more about not walking past what I considered to be an injustice and ensuring others might not suffer what is now commonly referred to as preventable moral injury. Anticipating that my application would be rejected out of hand, I was genuinely shocked to be informed that I had been selected.

Although this is just one isolated example, I am grateful to everyone who has ever doubted me. Each of them has played a part in pushing me to go that little bit further and tackle challenges head-on. But in those moments when I have had to work hard to put one foot in front of the other and keep moving forward, which does still happen from time to time, I have learned that there is always a way. It just requires us to slow down, take a deep breath and view the challenge from a different perspective; take it in context and look at the bigger picture, which may require some lateral thinking when there is no obvious path in the first instance.

This, we are told, is the very articulation of what neuropsychology has discovered about the human brain's needs in today's fast-paced world: putting things in context of space and time, seeing things from others' perspective and from a wider view, and taking a moment to re-engage our open-mindedness. This can be incredibly hard to do when we are stressed and don't feel like we have any time, but it is imperative that we get into the habit of thinking in this way in order to counteract chronic stress and cumulative trauma exposure.

Even today, embarking on a new or unfamiliar endeavour can still be daunting but, having built-up resilience over many years, I now feel overwhelming exhilaration and excitement, far more than fear, anxiety or stress.

I have learned to focus on the many opportunities that come from complex situations, rather than seeing primarily risk or threat – a natural, common and very human response. This approach has stood me in good stead, enabling me to grow and thrive rather than merely survive.

What it does not do, however, is prevent failure. That is not the point.

What it has done, and continues to do, is enable me to see the value in every situation and every outcome, whether positive *or* negative. And I can honestly say that I continue to learn far more from my failures, when I've really wanted to just give up, than when everything has gone to plan. Even though there have been many times that I was convinced there was no way through, I have always, without fail, got further than circumstances suggested I could, would or should.

Being selected at school to play rugby and row internationally are good examples of that. Both were hugely intimidating, but by putting myself out there and succeeding, at least in part, they opened a window into a world I'd never realistically imagined might be within reach. While I never won any world championship medals, it did sow the seed of an idea that perhaps there were other sports to which I might be more suited.

It wasn't until I joined the British Army that I was introduced to triathlon and duathlon and, after making it into the Army Triathlon Team and winning a national relay team event, I began to wonder if I might be able to experience once again the thrill of competing for my country. Yet, even this thought process scared me and had me wracked with doubt. Of the three triathlon disciplines, my running was OK and, although I have never been a proper cyclist, I found that I could pedal quite quickly when I put my mind to it. My Achilles heel, however, was swimming.

Having not swum competitively for 20 years, I was extremely rusty. With poor technique, I could never get quite enough oxygen, always feeling short of breath; not ideal for an aerobic sport. This meant (noting each Olympic-distance triathlon began with a 1,500-metre swim) that I always started the 40-kilometre cycle way down the field, having then to work doubly hard to make up ground so I would be in the mix for the final 10-kilometre run. Although I did have one or two wins in races that included shorter swims, it was clear that any aspirations I may have held to compete for Great Britain (GB) would not be realised if swimming was involved, so I adapted my plan, switching out swimming for an extra run and focusing instead on duathlon.

Here I found a better fit but, having raced at a few national team qualifying events and not won any of them, I allowed self-doubt to colour my thinking yet again and assumed that I would not make the cut for the GB age-group team. With all this happening during a busy phase of my military career, mid Army Pilots' Course, I allowed my training to tail off, focusing instead on flying.

I was genuinely surprised, therefore, to receive a letter from the British Triathlon Association (BTA) informing me of my selection for the World Duathlon Championships in France, less than a month away. Although the letter had been sent many weeks before, it had seemingly been lost or gone 'missing in action' in the army's internal mail system. Bloody typical!

I contacted the BTA immediately to learn if my lack of response meant that they had given my slot to someone else, half thinking that this might be the best outcome, as I was nowhere near fit enough for a race of this magnitude.

They hadn't. Shit!

I chose not to let on that I was woefully unprepared. Instead, I set about a panic fitness programme. The last thing I wanted to do was embarrass myself or the team.

The timing of the race was really not that ideal either, coming as it did the day after our course graduation ceremony (and party). Not wanting to miss out, I organised for my racing bike to be shipped to France without me so I could attend at least some of the graduation celebrations; the culmination of 18 months of intense training and stress. I would be lying if I said I didn't have a couple of drinks, but I *did* leave the party at 11 p.m., which gave me a few hours' sleep before my drive to catch the ferry to Calais, in time for a race start at 9.30 a.m. the next morning.

Arriving in France at about 7 a.m., I drove around Calais old town desperately looking for somewhere to buy breakfast. Finding only one shop open but still waiting on its pastry delivery, this was not the most auspicious start to my international duathlon career. Looking back, it was definitely one of those laugh or cry moments. Not for the first time, I chose to laugh. Hell, the rest of my preparation had been ridiculous, so this felt rather fitting and in keeping. Grabbing a single stale croissant from the previous day's stock, I headed off in search of my bike, which also proved to be a more difficult task than I'd anticipated. With international roaming for mobile phones yet to be commonplace back then, everything hinged on plans set before we had all left the UK. Initially, I could find neither my bike nor any other members of the GB team.

After nearly an hour of searching, I finally gained entry to the transition area. Thankfully, my friend Doug, also in the same age-group team and a fellow army officer and helicopter pilot, had made sure that everything was where it needed to be. After a quick change in the back of my car, I was ready, whatever the hell that meant.

Although this was not textbook preparation, as I stood on the start line, I had never felt more relaxed for any competition in my life. Despite this being a huge race (for me at least), my first world championship in a completely new sport, I felt incredibly calm. Even though I knew I would be competing against the very best athletes in the world, each one of whom would have prepared meticulously, I just felt at peace. It was surreal. I was so used to pressure (usually self-induced), routinely setting impossibly high expectations, but because so much of my preparation had been out of my control on this occasion, my mindset was completely different.

I was, for the first time that I can remember, kinder to myself. I'd never heard of the term self-compassion back then, but I realise now that I was applying it in practice, which is something all of us can do.

Did I still want to try my best and achieve a good result? Absolutely. But I also felt that just getting to the start line had been a challenge in and of itself, so everything from that point forward was a bonus. I would do my level best to just enjoy it.

So often, we are our own harshest critics and mistake self-compassion for self-indulgence, when the opposite is true. I would certainly never dream of talking to others in the language of my own, often illogical, or unreasonably negative, internal dialogue. I am learning (albeit I appear to be a slow learner) that when we show ourselves kindness, we open the channels for more positive, resilient and courageous options when faced with adversity. Constant self-criticism can be highly counterproductive and is, quite simply, unhelpful.

Since that race in Calais, I have often wondered how I would have felt if my preparation had been perfect. I am pretty sure that I would not have had the race of my life, as I did, achieving a personal best. And while a podium finish was never on the cards, I did manage a world ranking of 20th. I was buzzing. I had given everything and, despite a few moments when my mind was telling my aching, unprepared body that the pain would go away if I just stopped, I didn't.

I am certainly not advocating that to avoid self-doubt one should not train or prepare, but I did learn a valuable lesson about how to channel positivity, get in the flow and overcome the odds, even when they may not always be in your favour.

Despite making it into the national team again for the following year's competition, frustratingly, I was unable to improve my ranking despite training much harder, such is the way of competition. Sadly, although I didn't know it at the time, this would be the last time I would represent my country internationally, in sport at least; the bullet injuries sustained on Halloween a few years later put paid to my competitive sporting ambitions.

But recognising that most challenges take place well away from the sporting arena, is it possible to get in the 'zone', channel positivity and overcome self-doubt in everyday life? It is certainly possible but, from my own experience, it takes deliberate practice and effort. By committing to it, however, we enable more open thinking; our brains no longer encumbered by a sense of threat. Instead, we can learn to be present in an optimal state of enjoyment with what is going on around us. In sport, this is often described as being in a 'flow state';

when one is completely absorbed and engaged in the activity, fully focused and in tune with one's performance and environment.

I remember reading numerous stories of people talking of incidents when, for them, time slowed down. I had always wondered why and what happens in the moment as it was something I didn't experience until well into my thirties, after nearly ten years of military operations.

During my first major gun battle with the 'bees', time most definitely did not slow down. Rather, everything in those first few moments was absolute chaos, as the bullets whistled around us and my brain struggled to make sense of it and keep up with the speed of the rapidly evolving situation. It was only well after the fact that I was able to piece together the entire incident and understand what had happened.

In the heat of that first big battle, I was frustrated about why I hadn't just been able to click into a different gear and get everything right. It was only after some soul searching, as well as experiencing several similar incidents, that I realised there are some things for which no amount of training can prepare you. Until you're in the heat of the moment and feeling the pressure, emotion and confusion of the situation, it is hard to understand how it will affect you. That said, had I not been put through realistic training, something the military is pretty good at, things might well have been even more catastrophic.

What I needed to do was bank the experience and build on it, leveraging Dr Rick Hanson's 'HEAL' technique (introduced in Chapter 2), namely: **H**aving the experience; **E**nriching it with understanding; **A**bsorbing it into memory and thinking consciously about banking it so one can **L**ink to it when resilience might be needed in the future.

So, although it took some time for me to process the Halloween experience and getting shot, I have no doubt that the extensive conditioning we all went through helped me bounce back more quickly, both from self-doubt and internal recrimination.

Given the frequency of exposure to these types of events over my career, I noticed that, in some of the most chaotic situations, it did indeed feel as if time slowed down. The upshot of this was that, particularly when responding to incidents such as high-profile terrorist attacks, the more complex or confused the situation, the more I was able not only to cope and think but also to lead, and lead effectively.

While I was always conscious of the dangers of complacency, having built up my memory bank of valuable experience and resilience, I had found a place where the self-doubt so familiar to me melted away. These were my moments where I felt, when it mattered, that I was finally the right person in the right place at the right time.

Returning to our brain's memory system for a second, what happens to us as we leverage the reservoir and experience of resilience? Neuropsychologists have found that, essentially when something is not right, a part of the brain called the amygdala raises the alarm. Although small, it plays a central role in our emotional responses, including feelings like pleasure, fear, anxiety and anger. Additionally, the amygdala helps attach emotional content to our memories, which, in turn, determines how robustly those memories are stored. As soon as this happens, another area called the hippocampus then retrieves a memory of a similar situation, enabling us to be reminded that we've been here before and we know that it worked out well. This then gives us a sense of resolve that we have the capacity to deal with the current situation and helps mute the alarm, so we can get on with taking action without being overwhelmed by a stress response.

In my own experience, this really does work. During incidents later in my career, with bullets flying, explosions all around or casualties mounting, rather than being filled with a sense of panic or fear, I was overcome with a sense of calm, a clarity of purpose and thought that enabled me and my team to find a way through.

Long since retired from active duty and no longer required to run towards the sound of the guns, I have had space to think about the more testing times. In those hectic moments when I felt a welcome sense of calm – which to some might almost read like dissociation; something that can manifest with repeated exposure to trauma – I felt that I was able to reside in the gap between stimulus and response. By filtering out all the noise and chaos around me, triaging what was most important, it afforded me precious moments of awareness to consider the most appropriate action and outcome.

I've been fortunate to hold a variety of roles and had extensive opportunities to build resilience and navigate the many personal and professional challenges life has thrown at me. That said, apart from those early experiences performing in front of thousands as a child singer, the only other situations in which I have felt complete calm – an absence of self-doubt, fear of failure or a perception of failure – was in those hell on earth moments, where the stakes were highest and the situation was most dire.

Unfortunately, given that constantly putting oneself in harm's way is not entirely compatible with living a long life, I had to find ways to take these lessons and apply them to the other facets of life. Without realising it at the time, the skills I had learned were a culmination of years of exposure to, and then navigating solutions for, trauma. I had found a way to embrace uncertainty and, rather than fear the unknown, I made a conscious choice to tackle doubt head-on and relish the possibilities inherent in the unknown.

PRACTICAL TECHNIQUE: 'THE SECOND ARROW'

In this chapter we have explored what can happen when we get in our own way. When we do this, it is like there are two injuries: one caused by the arrow of the actual experience; the second inflicted by the arrow we unwittingly shoot ourselves through self-criticism or doubt. We can learn to avoid the second injury by taking a breath before we lurch into giving ourselves a hard time. This pause can enable us to deal with just the one arrow well enough to be able to move on.

Science and Thinking

Reward and self-compassion

Many of us utilise the brain's sense of reward by cultivating opportunities for its release through pursuing challenges (Bromberg-Martin et al., 2010), often involving the dynamic of being judged by others (Kedia et al., 2014). We find ourselves putting ourselves last. In the National Health Service (NHS) standard MBSR course (Mindfulness-Based Stress Reduction) being gentler on ourselves is the final step in the module. This step is so unpopular that many MBSR deliveries actually make the disclaimer that this final part of the training is optional. Especially for those in service professionally, thinking about others may come more naturally than being inwardly compassionate. Thankfully, there are practical exercises that can help and there is also the work of Rockman (2016) on self-compassion. Other resources include those offered by Buddhist neuropsychologists, such as Kristen Neff.

Self-doubt

Doubt is the false friend of curiosity and open-mindedness. Self-doubt is no different. There have been studies in the business world into how entrepreneurs (the very people who are likely to explore opportunities) deal with moments of self-doubt, or challenges to a sense of self-efficacy, and the key seems to be: accept it and move on. One study (Haines and Townsend, 2014) surmises, 'Entrepreneurs engage in an active process of transforming negative mental states by leveraging their intentionality, engaging in forethought, taking consistent action, and relying on the support of others.'

Moral injury

Within the emergency services and the military is a rapidly emerging and most welcome rhetoric around 'moral injury'. The concept of moral injury is well worth reading up on as many of us can relate to times when we have been put in positions that go against our moral code and have had to bear that conflict and carry on. Thanks to the work of many conscientious occupational and neuropsychologists (e.g. Williamson et al., 2022), we are learning more and more how to look after ourselves, especially in public service, where decisions are uncomfortable and the stakes for our self-worth are high. There are some very practical ways in which we can protect ourselves against moral injury, one of which is broadening our perspective on a situation, rather than contracting around an element which we think is to blame.

It's not uncommon to find ourselves saying (or overhearing others saying) in times of trouble, 'Maybe you need some space' (often accompanied with 'Oh, give it time' or – frustratingly sometimes – 'Time is a great healer'). This is all very well, but how do we actually do that? Fortunately, through Nobel Prize-winning work by John O'Keefe on the hippocampus (see: www.nobelprize.org/prizes/medicine/2014/advanced-information/) we now know that we can actually use our minds very pragmatically to genuinely cultivate a felt sense of a bigger picture. This means we can learn to take that which we are finding really hard and place it in a much bigger pot of experience. We can 'dilute' it. A good analogy for this is a teaspoon of salt. If we put a teaspoon of salt in a shot glass and drink it, the taste will be potent and all we might think about is the saltiness we can taste. However, if we were to place the exact same teaspoon amount in a bucket of water and drink from that bigger bucket, chances are that the salt would be barely detectable and our focus may be on the refreshing or bland quality of the water. Creating a bigger context around an experience can be done with playing with the space around it, expanding the area in which the experience sits and seeing that from different perspectives. This is referred to as cultivating an overhead or 'helicopter view', using our mind's eye and mapping out spaciousness around a pertinent situation graphically (Miller et al., 2020).

5

Never Giving Up

Learning Smart Compassion and Building Resilience Incrementally

'It does not matter how slowly you go, as long as you don't stop.'

Confucius, Chinese philosopher

Never give up!

Three simple words.

I often say this to my own family – and most of us will probably have said the same thing to close friends, children or colleagues at some point – as motivation to overcome whatever challenge they might be facing. Although simple words, acting on them can sometimes be hard to do.

I have often received such advice and, while it is easy to understand in principle why we should not give up, our minds can often play tricks on us when struggling in the moment. More than once my brain has suggested that the best course of action would be to quit, as happened during the race in Calais, long before my body has failed me.

How, then, do we defeat the negative voice in our head that appears, superficially at least, to offer a realistic or preferable alternative? Being able to listen to voices and thoughts and opinions as they arise, and then pause before responding, is key. But which thoughts are useful? Which are coming from a place that we understand, but may not necessarily help us go in the direction we want or need to? How do we counter the thoughts that promise immediate relief from whatever it is we are facing, such as 'Stop running and the pain will go away' or 'Just walk away; everyone will understand'?

Long story short, it's not easy, and to develop the skills or coping strategies takes time and practice; to learn to identify the warning signs and build the resilience and confidence to stay the course even when sometimes you cannot see a way through.

As Nelson Mandela said after his release from his long incarceration on Robben Island, 'It always seems impossible until it's done.' And he should know, having spent 27 years imprisoned by the apartheid regime, without any realistic chance of release, yet finding the strength not to lose hope; never giving up until the day he was free.

In my own experience, every time I have allowed myself to indulge in, even momentarily, an internal conversation about giving up, I have regretted it.

Every single time.

And on each occasion, once I'd defeated any negative impulses and seen the challenge through, I realised that all I had done in practice was to make my journey longer or the situation more difficult to resolve.

I recognise, however, that to keep going when the odds are against you is often easier said than done. But I have learned time and again that it always pays to keep doing just that, even if we do not succeed, very much in step with Confucius' teaching: 'It does not matter how slowly you go, as long as you don't stop.' Personally, no matter what the outcome, knowing that I gave my all has always afforded me an opportunity for learning – another piece in the resilience puzzle – something that quitting never would.

That said, I am not suggesting you ignore situations that present an obvious threat to life or limb. In such cases, where continuing blindly could do lasting damage to yourself or others, or open yourself to emotional or physical abuse, you must make a judgement call. In these scenarios, stopping does not at all mean giving up. Rather, it is the courageous, sensible choice and constitutes an important difference for all of us to grasp; stopping something for a good reason is not quitting something we are committed to because it is difficult. Being able to do this and know when it is the correct decision is executive function at its everyday best.

While I have faced a multitude of physical challenges during my sporting and military careers, the most traumatic situations I have had to deal with have been far more emotional and far more personal.

In Chapter 2, 'Child's Play', I gave a few glimpses into my troubled childhood, and how I vowed to protect my own children from difficult experiences. Therefore, to find myself, some 30 years later, in an equally devastating emotional and financial situation, this time as a parent rather than the child, was a shock, to say the least.

Paying almost every penny I earned every month to lawyers to help me fight for precious time with my daughter was never part of the plan; a set of circumstances I often struggled to see a way through and one that I felt virtually powerless to influence for many years. Yet I refused to give up – the consequences of doing so were unthinkable – and, after many difficult weeks, months, years, I did eventually find a way to get through it.

Did I emerge on the other side emotionally and financially battered, bruised and traumatised? Absolutely. But focusing on the long-term goal and maintaining the vision of a future that was full of hope and promise enabled me to roll with the punches, regardless of the difficulties along the way. In hindsight, even this extremely upsetting, stressful experience was valuable, as I learned lessons and built layers of resilience on which I still rely.

Is it possible that my own early trauma may have been a factor in how I was able to cope with the challenges I faced as an adult? Very possibly, but it can be hard to acknowledge how our own resilience can grow out of abuse, often because either we don't want to be seen as a victim (I certainly didn't and don't), or perhaps don't want to attribute any positive consequences to another's vile acts. Nonetheless, if we work with our experiences because we choose to, post-traumatic growth is ours for the taking.

But not all challenges – where giving up was an attractive option – were as viscerally personal or emotional. Many of them have been entirely self-inflicted: I have no one to blame but myself. Several of these opportunities for learning and reflection took place during the Covid-19 pandemic between 2020 and 2022. Because of international travel restrictions during that period, in order to be allowed to enter Australia and spend any time with my daughter, I endured two weeks at the start of every visit locked in a Sydney hotel room, unable to leave or, in my case, even open a window.

Although I know that many victims of this apparently draconian policy found the very act of being locked in a small room a challenge in and of itself, I always tried to look for the positives, no matter how small, rather than focus on the negatives. I kept in the forefront of my mind how fortunate I was to secure permission to enter the country at all, let alone numerous times; something many families were denied for nearly two years.

Once secured by New South Wales police, I established a daily routine, identifying simple things to look forward to: making a fresh coffee, exercising, reading or even just texting with or calling a friend. All the while, I remained laser-focused on the goal: being reunited with my daughter.

Nothing else mattered.

I've since learned that this focus and priming of the brain is known in neuroscience as 'cognitive control of attention', something that *can* be impaired in those with experience of trauma. Thankfully, in this case, being a father outweighed my experience of being the child of an abusive one, as I sought to galvanise my resources and execute a plan.

Giving up was not an option.

After surviving my first stint relatively unscathed (apart from being mildly traumatised by some truly awful food), I felt that I had wasted an opportunity to make a difference. All I had really done was work, and on European time, resulting in constant fatigue. So, hearing stories of the millions of people who were really struggling with enforced isolation and the concomitant lack of human contact, I made a pledge that I would, during any subsequent Covid-19 visits, endure a little discomfort to raise awareness of, and money for, several veterans' mental health charities close to my heart, including RBLI.

While I made this about other people, subliminally this was also key to my own resilience. Making time to know and understand what nourishes each of us is important. Working (or overworking) can sometimes be a welcome distraction, both constructive and enjoyable. Yet, at other times, it just doesn't hit the spot. Instead, when we feel absolutely depleted, the act of giving can enrich us and refuel our tank. This may at first seem counterintuitive, however, when making a conscious choice to give, we are actually telling ourselves on some level that we still have something *to* give, and, therefore, this is a quiet acknowledgement that we are going to be OK. What's more, we then feel the reward of knowing that others are more nourished because of us – the Buddhist concept of 'smart compassion' again.

To that end, for my next Sydney hotel lockdown I decided to run a marathon in my hotel room; large enough only for me to run eight paces before turning around . . . While I might well score highly on the compassion part, few agreed it was a particularly smart idea.

Although daunted by my now publicly declared plan (which meant I could not back out of it easily), the RBLI team was amazing. Securing a live interview on Sky News prior to setting off, together with several other media opportunities during and after the race, meant I had a growing community of supporters, most of whom thought I had clearly gone mad.

Apart from the challenge of running in such a small space and the lack of appropriate nutrition or proper training, the first 20 miles or so were bearable. Uncomfortable, yes, but bearable. Listening to news and current affairs podcasts on ×1.5 speed kept me going, and although the approximately 11,500 turns were tough on my knees and ankles, they put me in a trance-like state as I watched minutes and hours tick by.

Stupidly, however, as I approached the 26-mile mark (as donations continued to flow in), I told those following me online that if they kept donating, I would keep running.

Schoolboy error.

It was only after a further 6 (quite unpleasant) miles, during which I wanted to give up at every turn, I realised that a few friends were timing donations to keep me in the hurt locker. Although I wanted to keep going and raise as much money as possible, and despite feeling mentally strong, my body was starting to fail me. So, after just over 32 miles, I called it a day, having raised nearly £10,000. As I only ever intended to run a normal marathon rather than an ultra, I didn't consider this to have given up.

You would think that I might have learned my lesson from this event, but no. A few months later I ran the London Marathon dressed in an inflatable Tyrannosaurus Rex costume, to raise money for Afghan refugees who had been relocated to the UK after fleeing the Taliban. While the cause was noble, the positives that went with being cocooned inside a sealed plastic bag proved elusive. However, given how much suffering my Afghan brothers and sisters had endured and the resilience *they* had shown, meant that *my* discomfort was utterly inconsequential.

Not all the situations in which I've found myself questioning whether I could continue or should give up were as physical, yet they were no less scary or uncomfortable.

Although I wasn't that familiar with the military growing up, I do remember a television commercial from the early 1990s highlighting the experiences of an individual called Frank, who always seemed to be doing exhilarating things as part of his work in the army. While this didn't influence my decision to sign up, it certainly reinforced my view that if I was going to join the army, the number and type of experiences would make for an interesting and exciting life. Frank was a fictional character, but I related to that desire to try everything and learn new things whenever the chance arose, which included facing my fears head-on.

Being clear about what fazes us and what doesn't can be helpful – knowing one's aversions is just as crucial to resilience as following one's passions. Insights like these require a degree of self-awareness but are foundational in building our emotional intelligence.

One such opportunity to test this out saw me train to become a mountaineer. Even though I had never been keen on heights (though flying, parachuting or hanging out of helicopters never bothered me), I love the mountains and was keen to give it a try. As the climbing became more demanding and technically advanced, we had to learn to trust each other and our equipment implicitly. Any lapses in concentration could have serious consequences. Trust is a hugely valuable psychological resource for resilience; without it we'd be embarking on a potentially dangerous activity with a key weapon missing from our resilience armoury.

The training programme not only required us to learn summer techniques but also how to move safely on ice and snow. To that end, we headed up onto a glacier in the Swiss Alps so we could be taught how to navigate in small groups, a technique known as 'short roping'.

Most were split into teams of three – a single rope connecting them together – the idea being that if any one of us fell into a crevasse, the person or people left standing above ground would use ice axes and crampons to arrest the descent of their teammate, before helping him or her to climb back out. With an odd number of students in our group, I found myself roped only to our Swiss mountain guide. As a pair, it allowed us to move more quickly than the larger groups and, with his local knowledge, we led for much of the time.

Most of the ice felt solid as we progressed up the glacier, but it was clear that there were still deep crevasses just below the surface.

After crossing the main glacier without incident, the guide led me to the foot of a convex ice wall, which connected to a rocky ridge several hundred feet further up the mountain. At its base was a sinister-looking crevasse. Standing several feet back, I watched as the guide stepped carefully onto a narrow lip of ice jutting out about halfway across the mouth of the dark, yawning cavern beneath. Testing each step carefully before applying any weight, he signalled that it was strong enough to use safely. He then deftly crossed the remaining gap before scampering up the ice wall and out of sight.

Once in position, having attached an ice screw for my safety rope, he shouted for me to begin climbing. Heart in mouth, I placed my left foot gingerly into the footprint left by the guide moments before and, conscious that I was taller and heavier than him, I listened carefully for the slightest indication of weak ice beneath. Hearing nothing, I placed my right foot into the guide's second print. Again, no obvious signs or sounds to cause alarm, but, as I adjusted my weight to take the final step across the chasm, there was a sudden cracking beneath me and the entire lip on which I was standing sheared off, throwing me into the icy blue yonder.

Although it all happened in a split second, everything seemed to unfold in slow motion.

After falling about 10 or 15 feet, my backpack snagged on a lump of ice sticking out of the ice wall, which caused my legs to be thrown up in front of me. As my crampons connected violently with the opposite wall, I was able to gain enough purchase to bridge, albeit uncomfortably, just as the dynamic safety rope reached the full extent of its elasticity. My fall now arrested, I was left perching precariously as remnants of the ice ledge continued to clatter noisily to the bottom, several hundred feet below.

Scanning my surroundings, heart still thumping, what struck me immediately was how dark it was even just a few feet below the surface. My icy tomb was a beautiful palette of rich blues and greys, something I had never seen before. In this quiet moment, I sought to calm and regulate my breathing, which I hoped would both allow enough oxygen to my muscles to enable me to hold my position and help me clear my mind to think.

And then there was silence.

Once I had composed myself enough to begin planning my extraction, I thought perhaps I might hear colleagues at the surface, rushing to my aid and asking if I was hurt. Instead, all I could hear was raucous laughter some way above me. Assuming (correctly) that I wasn't going to get any help from them, I used my ice axe and crampons to climb slowly and rather amateurishly up and out. As I breached the surface and scrambled onto firmer ground, my 'friends' were still giggling among themselves, and even though adrenaline was still coursing through my veins, my body was already feeling bruised and battered.

Asking why they had not helped me, they apologised, but said it had been so funny to watch that they really couldn't help themselves, let alone me. Having stopped a safe distance behind to observe the crevasse crossing, they reported that when I vanished, it had looked very much like the way the cartoon character Wile E. Coyote used to fall after running off a cliff.

After finally climbing back up to the rendezvous with my now very grumpy guide, I explained what had happened, however, he showed little interest other than to tell me I shouldn't do it again and we were going to be late to the next rendezvous. Tough crowd.

We resumed our ascent and, reaching the top of the ice wall without further incident, the terrain became rocky as we prepared to head off along a knife-edge ridge. Before continuing, the guide repeated that it was imperative to stay alert as there was even less room for error if one of us lost our footing, with only two on the short rope. He made it clear that if he fell, I should immediately throw myself off the other side of the ridge to provide a counterbalance and prevent both of us being dragged to our deaths.

Scampering along the ridge behind him, freeing loose stones and rocks underfoot, I have rarely felt more alert in my life. There was no time to dwell on the dangers of the situation we found ourselves in. I just had to push through my fears, trust in the training and the equipment and try to enjoy the experience.

Having been extremely fortunate to be part of some wonderful teams in my life, I've learned that we all process emotions very differently. It is therefore incumbent on each of us, whether the leader or a follower, to remember that each of us will pick up on and react to environmental stimulation in diverse ways (and that's before we even begin thinking about other influences on resilience and trauma processing, such as age, genetics, neurodiversity or diet).

There have been occasions when I have felt strong or confident while some of my teammates have felt exhausted, full of doubt or unable to see a way through; and many times it has been the other way round. On that knife-edge ridge I certainly lacked confidence and, despite wearing my best game face, I was scared and not sure if I'd fail (or fall).

So, taking time to recognise the signs in yourself and in others, when you or they might be struggling, is an important part of leadership and teamwork; something we can all upskill. This is why I have included some practical tips at the end of each chapter – quick exercises to help our brains and bodies better face own challenges head-on.

During military pilot training, for some, the helicopter underwater escape trainer (HUET), known colloquially as 'the dunker', filled them with abject fear. However, being able to practise the drills required to exit from a helicopter, should it make a forced or unscheduled landing in water, was critical, and to refuse or fail to do so would mean deselection from the course. The stakes were high. If you've never seen the HUET contraption, it is essentially a metal mock-up of a helicopter cabin, suspended over a deep swimming pool, that can tilt, turn and roll in any direction, depending on the degree of disorientation desired as it hits the water.

The initial dunk routinely saw the helicopter remain upright and was completed with the hangar lights on. However, even in this relatively benign scenario, the speed at which it was possible to become disorientated was surprisingly high. As we passed each level, the scenarios got more advanced. And to ensure that none of us became too comfortable, the staff made us change seats every time. Forcing us to reorientate for each scenario was designed to test and develop our mental agility and ability to make decisions under pressure; brain foggy and lungs screaming. After eight or nine dunks, we moved from daylight, upright ditching to a full roll, upside down in the dark. As unpleasant as this sounds, getting through it as a team provided us with an opportunity to bond. Providing each other with encouragement and support (as along with some good-natured teasing) helped to silence any voices in our heads that might be telling us to quit.

Training like this, as well as other equally unpleasant tests, reinforced the requirement to work as a team and support those who were scared or battling demons about quitting. We could only imagine the catastrophic implications if any of us found ourselves facing this for real. In those situations, giving up would absolutely not be an option, so we had to learn instead how to recognise risk, face our fears and overcome them.

PRACTICAL TECHNIQUE: 'THE BIGGER PICTURE'

In this chapter we have explored what it can feel like to take life's challenges a bit at a time, step by step. This can be hard when we have contracted around something about which we are slightly obsessing, and which has become so big in our minds that we can't seem to break it down. What can really help in these situations is to make this 'thing' smaller another way: by shrinking it. We can do this by deliberately putting it in context of a bigger picture: recognising how big the world is, how long a life we have and where we have come from in our existence. When we take a minute to do this, that which seemed to be the be-all and end-all (perhaps for good reason at the time) can become more manageable.

Science and Thinking

Internal conversations about giving up

Testing a feeling or an emotion to see if it really has weight and volume is a skilful thing to do. It's possible to practise this turning towards something negative (e.g. the desire to quit, a pain, a difficult emotion) while maintaining our stability and not taking that path of thinking. Science has shown this to be helpful with pain relief and distress, making us physically, as well as psychologically, stronger (Kober et al., 2019). Mark Twain once said, 'I've lived through some terrible things in my life, some of which actually happened.' Buddhism predated today's neuroscientific and evolutionarily biological understanding of a negativity bias (Rozin and Royzman, 2001) by having at its very core the concept of 'aversion'. What are known as the Four Noble Truths reflect on the essential conviction that, as humans, we need to accept negativity, suffering and our aversion to it as being part of life – in order to prevent it from taking over our thinking. A very logical step-by-step technique to help us with this is the skill called RAIN, to which we have already referred.

Post-traumatic growth

Post-traumatic growth is now a clinical concept (Calhoun and Tedeschi, 2014), which gives hope to many who have suffered a sense of going backwards or diminishing – being less than they were – because of the adverse circumstances in which they found themselves. Psychologists have long explored the relationship between imagining the future and resilience, and also, on the flip side, trauma. Having a firm view of the future can help us prime our brain and galvanise our resources (Lombardo, 2007). Having an unstable concept of the future is also known to be a prominent feature of adult life following childhood trauma (Ratcliffe et al., 2014).

Smart compassion

In neuroscience, smart compassion is one of the most sophisticated executive functions of our prefrontal cortex, the newest part of our brain, and yet it is steeped in ancient traditions that predate technology (Jaeger and Gonpo, 2021). In practical terms, smart compassion is not a case of blindly opening ourselves to the care of others suffering, but is a means by which we can recognise what hurts others and be there for them in ways which keep us safe and can actually contribute to our own well-being. It means creating boundaries, acknowledging our own response to others' suffering as a witness and utilising subtle compassion to contradict feelings of unnecessary apprehension or aversion to others. We can use visualisations of there being a window between us and those who are suffering, or the simple reminder that, 'as much as I can feel this for someone, this suffering is not mine' (Miller, 2022).

Recognising vibes in others

There are practical exercises that we can undertake to help our brains and body naturally pick up on the vibes and feelings of others. More and more, neuroscience is demonstrating how working with our vagus nerve can really assist with this. For more about the pragmatic approach to upskilling yourself using vagal tone, look up work by Stephen Porges (Polyvagal Theory, 2011). Research into the vagus nerve in neuroscience has brought a plethora of practical techniques to tune up this wiring, which can enable us to become calmer, astute, more regulated and tuned in to others around us (Miller, 2022). Techniques for stimulating this nerve include: taking a long exhale, discrete disclosure (offering someone a demonstration of trust by disclosing something relatively private or confidential), friendly gestures of eye contact, smiling, nodding and gesticulating affectionately or casually with the arms, an open posture and specific physical activities (such as slow breathing exercises, chanting, music therapy, stretching, massage, cold water immersion, fasting and sleeping on the right side of the body).

6

Relationship Breakdowns

Seeing the Bigger Picture and Moving Beyond Pain and Hurt

'We too, like trees, can shake off our dead leaves and begin again.'

A. Y. Greyson, poet

Having lost more than 60 friends and colleagues killed in action during my military career, with many hundreds more wounded or left with life-changing mental or physical injuries, I feel extremely fortunate to have made it through relatively unscathed. But every funeral, memorial or ramp ceremony (saying goodbye to a fallen comrade at an airport as they begin their journey home) that I've attended has left an indelible emotional mark.

Witnessing the coffins of fellow British, American, Canadian, Australian, Kiwi and Afghan soldiers, colleagues and friends wrapped in their nation's colours – or watching flags being folded ceremoniously – are slow-motion videos I can still recall as if they took place yesterday.

Yet, despite the tragedy, horror and loss I've experienced or observed, I have always found a way to view the world fundamentally through a positive lens, looking for opportunities for growth or joy in even the most challenging of situations.

In the case of my own combat trauma – as shocking as it was – perhaps because we all ran willingly towards the sound of the guns (literally) in the full knowledge that there was a very real chance we might pay the ultimate price, I have, so far at least, found a way to process it all without much conscious effort. This alone is something for which I will be forever grateful, given the number of veterans whose daily lives continue to be impacted by their service experiences, even decades later.

However, the same cannot always be said for personal trauma, particularly when it comes to relationships. During my childhood, as my parent's marriage lurched from one crisis to another there was little, if anything, I felt I could do to influence the outcome. Although this dynamic was not unexpected, it didn't make it any less unsettling, uncomfortable or upsetting.

Strong, healthy relationships form the backbone of society, but it's unrealistic to expect that all will be as positive or endure in the same way as we mature and evolve. And each will vary considerably depending on their nature and the dynamics of the parties involved: family, social, professional and, of course, romantic. But over and above the importance of interpersonal relationships in their own right, they are also critical at a more micro level, in terms of our own brain development and cognitive resilience.

As a child I was blessed with an incredibly strong group of friends, primarily by dint of my involvement in multiple sports teams at school. And, despite my challenging and sometimes disruptive behaviour, they stuck with me then and continue to be hugely important and positive influences in my life today. Although most didn't realise it at the time, they became my primary support group, from whom I drew strength and on whom I relied for a sense of belonging. So, despite my parents' overwhelmingly negative relationship, I was, thankfully, able to spend time with these amazingly kind, generous friends and, by extension, their families, too. It was with them that I learned the right lessons about relationships and what it means to be respectful, loving and tolerant, which, for the first time, I realised could and should exist unconditionally.

Early familial relationship lessons notwithstanding, almost every romantic relationship I have had has been overwhelmingly positive and whenever one has run its course, as some undoubtedly have, I've always tried to separate on good terms and remain friends. Maybe because of the sum of my experiences and the number of friends, colleagues and family members I've lost over the years, almost all far too soon, I do believe that life is too short for there to be bad blood or animosity. That said, if abuse, mistreatment, coercive control or manipulation have been evident or a core feature of a relationship, it's appropriate to make a clean break, if that is possible.

Mercifully, there have been few such occasions, but when I failed to spot what was happening around me, when unfolding events caught me completely by surprise, I was knocked sideways. At such times I had to leverage every ounce of resilience I'd built up and try to navigate a way through.

Perhaps what shocked me most, however, on those few occasions when a relationship spiralled out of control was the speed with which I was transported back to my childhood. Feeling, as an adult, the same sense of being unable to positively influence an outcome was unsettling and disconcerting; as if I was playing chess, but the person across the table was playing an entirely different game, the rules for which had not been shared and kept changing without warning.

Break-ups can be difficult and traumatic at any age, but when children are involved it multiplies the complexity and emotional trauma. That has, sadly, been my experience and despite all the other extreme trauma in my professional life to which I have been exposed, the parenting challenges I have faced have been the most emotionally traumatic, bar none.

As a relatively low-paid government employee, finding myself needing hundreds of thousands of pounds in legal fees to battle to be in my child's life was not something I ever thought would happen to me – a financial and emotional nightmare that meant, in reality, I could not afford to live. At best, I just existed. Eating only one or two meals a day for several years, I needed every penny not spent on surviving to pay for lawyers or court costs so I could stay in the fight. To that end, and given the parlous state of my finances, I saw no alternative but to volunteer, soldier that I was, for every operational deployment going. Despite the obvious risk to life, I would at least be housed and fed, two things that made a huge difference in my being able to keep going.

Being able to extricate myself from my own experience and see the bigger picture of wider need was, I found, a significant motivating factor. It may be that my military career made me aware of the enormity of the scale at which human suffering and challenge can exist, and my own by default became somewhat more manageable (even if only temporarily) as a result. In neuropsychology, I have learned that this is referred to as 'allocentric' processing and the opposite (less helpful) processing style is called 'egocentric'. Just as it sounds, egocentric processing reinforces the view of oneself. Conversely, allocentric processing encourages us to appreciate relationships between other things around us, helping us to gain perspective and see the world through different eyes; something that's particularly important where children are concerned. So, despite the immediate challenges, I did my best to remember that there were certainly others in more difficult circumstances than me and that I should try to focus on the bigger picture.

Statistically, there are a high number of cases globally in which children are negatively impacted by relationship breakdowns and life trajectories are altered as a result. Parents often forget, or sometimes simply ignore, the impact of separation and divorce on their children; particularly impacts that are not solely emotional. Separation, even when amicable, can affect children psychologically, physically and academically. One study I read suggested that there could be a 16 per cent increase in the risk of behavioural problems if a child is between 7 and 14 years old when their parents get a divorce. Another suggested that children of divorced or separated parents are up to twice as likely to live in poverty or engage in 'risky sexual behaviour' as they get older, and another estimated that children from divorced parents have an 8 per cent lower probability of completing their schooling, a 12 per cent lower probability of college or university attendance, and an 11 per cent lower probability of completing their degree. Numbers like these scare me witless.

I absolutely adore being a father and, while my parenting journey has not been without its difficulties, I would not change it for the world. No matter how emotionally, physically or financially draining the experience has been, the effort and every pound or dollar expended to be there for my daughter and for her to spend time with my family has been worth every precious minute. With this being my reality, I have had to accept that my life is now defined by when and how we can enjoy 'Daddy-daughter time'.

Flying for over 24 hours to Australia, spending only a few hours on the ground and taking the same flight in reverse that same day (often in the same seat!) several times a year, to ensure she gets time with her British family is exhausting, but we make it work as best we can, despite the logistical, financial and other obstacles.

During the Covid-19 pandemic, the geographical separation between us was particularly challenging. Over and above restrictions put in place by the Australian government, several carefully planned, government-approved trips from Australia to the UK were refused within hours of our planned departure; deeply upsetting both for my daughter, for me and my family. This meant that I had little choice but to travel and stay there instead, no matter the cost. As time dragged on, with the hotel quarantine clock ticking slowly, I tried to focus on the many parents or family members in far worse situations, either unable to travel at all or for whom being in such isolation would be a nightmare.

Although I had not consciously thought about how being a parent would change me, I have found it to be a very helpful way to connect with others.

As a direct consequence of not being able to afford to live in the UK during the height of my legal efforts to defend my daughter's rights to have both parents in her life equally, or as fully as possible, I spent nearly four years in Central Asia. While hazardous in the extreme, I had some amazing experiences, making many lifelong friends in the process. But in places and situations such as the ones in which I found myself, it can be hard to make connections when the culture is so dramatically different from one's own. However, rather than focusing on the differences in language, country or religion, I would always try to strip away any unnecessary or unhelpful cultural baggage to enable us to find ways to connect quickly and authentically. And having gone through a significant relationship trauma, I felt a new sense of openness. Gone were any barriers; gone the facades. As a result of my humbling marriage experience, I was able to make connections with increased humility. Although a soldier, I was first and foremost a father.

This mindset enabled me to meet my local contacts and colleagues as fellow parents and family men, rather than as a Western military officer and a foreign general or government minister. No matter how different the environments and cultures, when working with other like-minded people fatherhood was a topic around which we could often immediately find common ground. Taking time to learn about the importance of family to them and how specifically it differed or manifested itself in their culture was always time well spent, and allowed us to connect and build trust fast, father to father.

Importantly, this was not a charade – I believed in what I was doing – and it worked. And because my daughter was always in my thoughts, it was an aspect of my life I was happy to share, with passion and real authenticity. This was not, however, in line with official guidance.

During numerous pre-deployment training courses prior to operational tours of duty, I listened to countless instructors outline the topics that should remain 'off limits' when meeting with locals, including politics, religion and family. The logic, according to the military instruction manual at least, was that these topics were just 'too sensitive' and that to engage in conversation about any of them could cause offence. Additionally, sharing private or personal information might expose us to greater risk.

Personally, I believed this advice was misguided: I had some of the richest and most rewarding conversations of my life, precisely *because* I was willing to engage in these topics. And given the fact that many conversations in less developed countries begin with being asked about one's family, even if you are a stranger, it seemed odd to me to ban or discourage such conversations that had the power to connect, break down barriers and potentially build trust. Therefore, I made the decision that, on the balance of 'value versus risk', extending the hand of humility in fatherhood was more valuable for my ongoing resilience and outweighed any potential risk to my immediate safety.

When asked about my own family, I was always very candid about being separated from my child and how challenging that had been, explaining that our time together since her birth amounted only to days and weeks, rather than months or years; something most of them genuinely struggled to comprehend. Although the issues I continue to face in that regard were, and remain, alien to most of them, and indeed to most parents, every one of them showed genuine empathy and demonstrated a desire to support and understand.

My willingness to show vulnerability, I believe, also helped significantly in breaking down barriers and building trust with even the most intransigent of partners, enabling us to achieve far more together as a result.

So strong was the connection we built, by beginning with an open and honest foundation, that several senior Afghans still refer to my daughter as their 'niece' and some of my Afghan 'brothers' have even told their sons that, should anything ever happen to them, they must listen to the guidance of 'Uncle Ash'! Some also still insist on sending gifts for their 'niece', to ensure that she knows that her extended family is thinking of her and to maintain the connection to a culture that they see as being hers as much as theirs. I love that.

While some of my international partners operated in ways I will never understand completely, or can condone, when you strip away all other baggage they were also just parents trying to do the best for their children. Something none of my local colleagues (particularly those brought up in strong familial cultures) understood, however, was how contact with a child could be restricted. As such, when they understood that I was able to have only a single, short Skype call every two or four weeks, they became my daughter's greatest champions and would do anything to ensure that these brief, precious events went ahead regardless of how their timing, over which I had no control, impacted on our official meetings.

Invariably, the calls took place on Saturday or Sunday evening in Australia, which was in the middle of the first or second working day of the week in many places where I was deployed. This could have been an issue given the seniority of the officials with whom I often met, but their understanding meant that even senior government ministers would kick me out of their offices to ensure that I could get back to my base in time to read a bedtime story or catch up on all the latest kindergarten gossip.

The empathy and kindness of those locals, operating under considerable pressure themselves in various conflict zones, was extremely generous. For them to have protected and, in many cases, prioritised my time with my daughter was vital for my resilience. It showed me I was not alone in my endeavour.

On one occasion, a sweltering day during a summer deployment, the deputy minister ended our meeting abruptly and ushered me from his office. He cited the congestion as the reason, meaning that I'd need to leave immediately if I was to navigate Kabul traffic and make my call on time.

As my linguist, driver and I left the ministry, it was clear that the journey was indeed going to be slow. After ten minutes of limited progress, I became increasingly nervous about missing the start time.

After nearly 20 minutes, we had barely moved. It was clear to me that if I stayed in the vehicle there was no chance that I would make it.

Given a recent experience of losing the chance to speak with my daughter (when a terrorist attack meant I had been a few minutes late joining), I made an emotional, rather than strictly rational, decision.

Looking at my map of the city, I estimated that the nearest coalition base was only about 1.5 miles from where we were, so I decided to get out of my armoured vehicle and run the rest of the way. That would, I felt, give me a fighting chance to get to a workable Wi-Fi signal in the headquarters compound. I would then be able to grab a quick conversation with my little girl before she went to bed.

Donning my helmet, grabbing rifle and backpack, I leapt out of my air-conditioned armoured cocoon and began running.

I realise that this came at quite some risk (hence some embarrassment now that I allowed my emotions to take over), but I hoped that any insurgents would be so shocked to see a coalition soldier running through the streets that, by the time they realised what was happening, I would be out of sight and safe from attack or kidnap.

After surprising the security guards at the headquarters' main gate, arriving without a vehicle and dripping with sweat, I gained entry and sprinted the final few hundred yards to the cafeteria. I connected to the open Wi-Fi network at the second attempt and logged in. Although I was less than two minutes late for the call, nobody was there. My heart sank.

So I waited.

And waited.

And waited.

After 30 minutes of repeatedly calling and then emailing to ask if everything was OK, but getting nothing in response, I began to worry that perhaps something awful might have happened. I had no way of knowing, so I stayed there, on tenterhooks, in the hope that I might still get to speak to my daughter, even if only for a few minutes, or at least to get confirmation that everyone was well and that there hadn't been an accident.

After almost five hours, and several cancelled meetings later, I was forced to admit defeat and turn off my computer. Thankfully, nothing untoward had happened to my daughter, or to me during my dash for Wi-Fi, but it's an example of how far I will go to be there for her, despite obstacles in my way.

Given the cocktail of pressures, I had some dark periods. There were times when, given the emotional and financial impact of the actions of others, I did struggle to see a way through. But despite my personal challenges and the risks inherent in multiple deployments, the feeling of doing important work – making a positive difference – helped considerably.

It was in these moments that the love and support of friends made the difference. The friends who would not take 'no' for an answer and would continue to check in on me, even when I didn't respond because of the hole I was in. I was particularly touched by those who were not even my closest friends at the time; in other words, they were not the friends I'd expected to show interest, yet they proved the most tenacious in making the time to see if I was all right.

Strong relationships require work and so I continue to work on being a better friend, partner and parent by stripping away all those smaller, inconsequential things that often take up too much of our time, focusing instead on the things that really matter.

Making a conscious effort to be open, to love and to smile every day can make a big difference.

Accepting also that there are so many things over which we have no influence or control means that I no longer expend unnecessary time and energy on them. By making a conscious decision to just let them go, I've found that the negative energy that often comes with them also dissipates rapidly.

While this just seemed to me to be a sensible thing to do, the art of letting go also has scientific roots in psychology as well as neuroscience. By reducing the energy spent on negative thought processes, we release energy that can be used for more balanced views, which fosters open-mindedness; clearly something that could prove critical for those facing significant challenges, where resilience is being tested to the limit. Despite the 'letting go' effort being a work in progress, requiring routine attention, the more I practise the approach, the more I see the good; something we can all do.

PRACTICAL TECHNIQUE: 'THIS IS NOT ME'

In this chapter we have explored what it feels like to deal with conflict, neglect and disconnect from others, as we find ourselves meeting one person after another and navigating different dynamics each time. Our brains and bodies have evolved to connect to others, so it's hard when we find disconnect. Sometimes, though, it's necessary to acknowledge that we are different to others, especially if they undermine our values and sense of who we are. When someone presents themselves in a way you don't naturally find comfortable, a very empowering (and yet soothing) approach is to say to oneself, 'OK, so this is *not me*.' There is no judgement or betrayal here, just a healthy way of retaining one's best self and keeping going.

Science and Thinking

Interpersonal relationships

If we appreciate that we see things differently from others, it is not a great leap to understand that we can see things differently from how we ourselves may have done so before, and why. There is much research out there to demonstrate why we can change how we view the world (e.g. Siegel, 2001) but, perhaps more importantly, there is a growing wealth of practical information that shows us how to cultivate this flexibility as a skill, which is to the great benefit of those of us who practise the simple techniques regularly. A great book that talks to the reader about how our brains can think differently, and which includes practical exercises, is Rick Hanson's Neurodharma *(2020). If you want to root your adventure in why brains evolve and why we need to help ours to evolve to improve our relationships, work by Yuval Noah Harari (2015) is an inspiring and grounding read. He reminds us that it is through our understanding and ability to relate to others that we are thought to have developed as a species.*

Repeating relationship dynamics

To find oneself in relationships where previous dynamics might repeat themselves can be disconcerting, but take heart: our brains are wired to be efficient and, if we do sense early signs of attachment dynamics with which we are all too familiar, it might be that our brain does not sound a signal for alarm because it knows from experience what to do. This has been researched in-depth in relation to attachments (Bartholomew, 1993), and there are also practical ways to address such situations.

*It can be tough when we have a sense of relationships playing out in front of us in the same old (sometimes negative) ways and we can feel powerless and even fatalistic at times, but it needn't be the case. Just being able to catch your mind starting to go down that road of thinking is a positive step – and a major one – towards resilience and the rewriting of our story, but only if we choose to do something with that noticing. As we have mentioned before when discussing the STOP technique (**S**top, **O**bserve, **T**ake a breath and then **P**roceed), stopping for a second is an essential way to halt what we may perceive as inevitable. When proceeding, establishing a boundary between yourself and the other person can be helpful, just to give yourself some space to think independently and in a non-reactive way, breaking the link to previous patterns of behaviour or thinking.*

Once we have paused, this opens up more availability for us to consider other ways to cultivate more helpful thinking; other directions in which to steer our brain. For example, do we need to distance ourselves from the other person in terms of reminding ourselves we are different from them? (We have talked before about the 'This is not me' technique). Do we need to take a moment to look after ourselves and show ourselves some self-compassion (such as fitting our own oxygen mask before helping others, as we have mentioned previously)? Or can we just accept that, for the moment, we don't know what is actually going on (befriending that idea of not knowing, accepting that it's not always up to us to understand absolutely everything), also mentioned previously?

Maintaining connections

The ability to find connection in circumstances in which many of us would be overwhelmed by a sense of loss after the breakdown of a relationship is key to resilience, physically as well as mentally. There is now a formidable body of research (Cardona and Andrés, 2023) that demonstrates just how damaging social isolation can be for the immune system and cognitive decline, and how maintaining social bonds and a learning trajectory can protect us long into later life. There are many inspiring initiatives out there that have been established in order to help members of the emergency services and the military support each other, and to protect those who serve from social isolation from bodies such as Oscar Kilo in policing, the mental health charity MIND, Combat Stress, The Royal Foundation of the Prince and Princess of Wales, March on Stress and TITEN (from Cambridge Resilient Research Ltd).

The art of letting go

The art of letting go has also entered into modern discourse around resilience. When we think about something again and again it becomes physically wired into our neural networks, mainly because the brain has developed first and foremost to be efficient (Doidge, 2007). This is great if we are practising a new skill, but not so great if we are thinking unhelpful thoughts. This wiring is also known as 'positive neuroplasticity' and is based on the Hebbian theory of 'when neurons fire together, they wire together', or in other words: 'where the thoughts go, the energy flows'. If we can learn to redirect our thinking in more constructive, rational ways (Hanson et al., 2023) and to let go of less helpful trains of thought, this leaves us in a strong position for resilience and happiness with life exactly how it is, without waiting for things to change around us to make us feel better. A very simple, practical step is to develop a way of thinking that keeps you at a little distance from how you feel. Rather than thinking to oneself 'I feel angry' or 'I am overwhelmed' or even 'I'm so excited I could pop!', we can neutralise the phrases to: 'There is anger', 'There is overwhelm' or 'There is excitement'. Even by saying this silently in one's mind, we can feel the relief of the objectivity for a second so we can ground ourselves and take it less personally and take a moment. In that more liberated, calmer space we can often find new ideas, new hope or new resolve. Try it. Even if you find yourself thinking as you read this, 'This sounds like a load of . . .', try 'There is scepticism', and see if you can sense some room for a bit more open-mindedness or even subtle amusement about how your brain takes you where it does.

7

Recovery and Post-Traumatic Growth

Understanding Trauma Processing

'Never be ashamed of a scar. It simply means you were stronger than whatever tried to hurt you.'

Anonymous

After experiencing my first significant battlefield trauma on that fateful Halloween night, I really didn't know how the incident might affect me, not least because of my own injuries. There was a lot to process.

The first 24 hours, in particular, proved to be a rollercoaster of emotions and passed by in a bit of a blur.

After speaking with my mother to let her know I would be returning home for surgery, the next call I made was to my long-term ex-girlfriend. Although we had separated about a year earlier, she knew me better than anyone and I really wanted to hear her voice. Being seen and understood, having a shared context and frame of reference, can be a cornerstone of resilience in adverse situations and experiences of the upsetting, unusual and bizarre (of which there were plenty). In times like these we need a base, something to ground us and give us a sense of perspective. At that moment she provided all of this.

I had up to this point managed to keep everything together, but as I stood alone on the roof of our base, looking out over the city, I was overcome with emotion and burst into tears. I told her that we had been involved in an incident and that one of my colleagues, who had been just behind me, had been killed and that I and three others had been wounded. As all my adrenaline had evaporated by this point, when I explained further that two more bullets and some grenade shrapnel had ripped through my backpack just behind my head, the reality of how lucky I had been began to dawn on me.

With a military background herself, she knew instinctively what I was going through and provided exactly what I needed in that moment by just being there. She was someone I trusted implicitly and gave me a much-needed connection to my 'normal' or 'home' life, far away from the horrors of the battlefield. Even though she listened more than she spoke, just having someone for whom I didn't have to wear a mask or hide how I was really feeling was incredibly valuable, aiding me with my critical transition, as I began to process what had happened to me and my team.

Although I wanted and needed to be strong for them (a team into which I was a relative newcomer), in that call I let the tears flow, something I have no shame in admitting, and it provided a much needed and physiologically beneficial release of tension. Yet, this kind of raw emotion was something that all of us generally kept to ourselves, such was the nature of the conversation about mental health at the time, not just in the military but in wider society, which was not particularly helpful.

When the body continues to hold the residual tension of a stress response to immediate threat, bad things can happen physically (in terms of blood pressure, gastro-intestinal issues and cardiovascular disease) and cognitively (burnout, dissociation, hypervigilance, memory impairment and compromised situational awareness). Being able to release tension and distress, and process experiences each time – in order to reset the body and brain – is the only way to avoid damage to our systems. We all need that release from time to time.

Additionally, neuroscience tells us that the language centres in our brain go 'offline' when we are in an acute stress response, simply because if we are under threat, we need to act; we don't have time to chat about it. So, it is useful if we don't give ourselves a hard time for not being able to communicate brilliantly after a fright, but to let the volume of the alarm bell reduce and gently start the process of talking (about anything) to reconnect. Once this process has begun, the brain typically takes over and helps us facilitate processing difficult experiences by making sense of them and therefore turning off the alarm. This helps regulate the body's response to the stress and protects our physical health.

Back at our patrol base, once the initial shock had worn off, conversations with the leadership team focused instead on the practicalities of what would be needed for us to recover fully, or at least enough for me and my team to be allowed back in the fight. However, I did not make any time to consider what, if any, emotional healing might be necessary.

In the days after the incident, as the medical team planned our repatriation to the UK for additional surgery, my overarching concern was leaving my teammates. I'd read that, for some, being removed from the combat zone too soon makes it harder to process the experience. Yet this decision was out of my hands. As Ed and I packed our things, I hoped it would only be for a few weeks, but neither of us knew for sure.

Once onboard an ageing RAF Vickers VC10 for our aeromedical evacuation flight, Ed and I were offered canvas stretchers, but we declined because they didn't look very comfortable, stacked as they were, three high and with very little room to move. However, when a RAF medical evacuee was unable to fit into his allocated stretcher, I was given the chance to switch. I agreed to give it a try and I'm glad I did. After the duty medic administered painkillers and a muscle relaxant, I was strapped in and have no other recollection of the flight home until I was helped off the plane back at RAF Brize Norton.

After arriving in the UK, arrangements were made for each of us to transfer to the amazing NHS and military team at Birmingham's Selly Oak Hospital (on whom the military came to rely heavily for nearly two decades). In my case, not only did one of the country's best orthopaedic surgeons agree to perform my knee surgery, but he also offered to work over the weekend so that my operation could take place as soon as possible, aware that patients like me tended to be quite demanding in their desire to get back to work.

In his expert hands, there was little to be worried about, but as I lay in pre-surgery, I still found myself shaking uncontrollably. I began to overthink everything that could go wrong if the bullet in my left knee could not be easily removed. I had already been warned about the likelihood of nerve damage, but I was more concerned about not being able to run again. Although I've never been a natural runner, I had always found solace on the road. Therefore, the idea that I might not be able to just throw on some running shoes whenever I felt like it, wherever in the world I found myself, worried me.

Whereas the operation to remove the bullet in my right thigh had been carried out under a local anaesthetic, this one would require a full general. The nurses did their best to reassure me that all would be fine, as the anaesthetist began to inject the cold, white, yoghurt-like fluid into the cannula in my arm. At the same time, another nurse drew an arrow on my leg with a red Sharpie to indicate where the bullet lay, but I could see that it was in the wrong place. I tried to tell her, but just then the anaesthetic hit me with full force; I could only mumble garbled nonsense, before passing out.

After being brought round, initially I couldn't feel my leg. Panic rising, I feared that they had inadvertently severed all the nerves or amputated my leg with a good chance (given the issue with the red Sharpie) that they'd also got the wrong one. Please God, no.

Thankfully, while the nurse had indeed made a mistake (the original arrow had been crossed out!), the operation had been a success.

The surgeon came to see me in recovery and reassured me that all had gone as well as he'd hoped. But he did warn me there would probably be some loss of feeling, given that both the bullet and his incisions had damaged nerves. He hoped, however, that this would be only temporary. And with extensive soft tissue and ligament damage above the knee joint, he insisted that I start rehabilitation as soon as possible, not least to prevent unhelpful scar tissue, which might further reduce movement.

Once discharged, I headed home and tried to keep busy, but it was hard to be stuck back in the UK, knowing that my teammates were still risking their lives on a nightly basis, thousands of miles away.

This was not primarily an issue of FOMO (although it was hard to be sidelined) but, rather, the concern that they were continuing with dangerous missions, several team members short.

Friends tried to keep me entertained and I probably did a lot more partying than was sensible, making the most of having survived, while coming to terms with the loss of Mike.

Not long after getting home from hospital I was out in a local nightclub, dancing awkwardly on my crutches, when I received an unexpected phone call; number withheld. Although a little worse for wear, hearing the voice of my surgeon on the other end sobered me up rapidly as he told me, in a serious tone, that he'd reviewed the deep tissue swabs results and that I must get to a pharmacy as soon as possible. He explained that the laboratory analysis had picked up the presence of both *Escherichia coli* (*E. coli*) and another form of *Enterobacter*. This meant little to me at the time, but what I did manage to decipher was that the situation was serious enough for me to need antibiotics right away. The last thing I needed were complications that might further delay my rehabilitation and redeployment.

Then came Mike's funeral. I put on a suit and Ed, Paul and I drove down to meet the family and pay our respects.

Emotionally, I struggled.

This was the first time I had been close to Mike since we'd made entry to the compound just a few weeks before. Although I just about managed to remain composed for the service, when the mourners were asked to come up individually on their way out and stand with the coffin to say a final goodbye, I was overwhelmed. It was then that the full force of what had happened in those few short seconds on Halloween hit me.

Facing Mike's coffin, alone, I felt very exposed. Tears were now streaming down my cheeks. Knowing that I was about to come face-to-face with his family, who would no longer benefit from his smile and his laugh, hit me like a freight train.

Would they be angry? Would they blame me? *Should* they blame me? Probably. I was, after all, the assault commander.

This was all very real and the family's journey on a cycle of grief was only just beginning. There would be many tough weeks and months ahead in a process that needed to run its course.

Whether due to my own sense of shame, or indicative of the way I perceived I should behave, I was embarrassed about getting so emotional in public and went straight to the church bathroom to wipe away the tears. After pulling myself together, I met some of Mike's friends and colleagues, as well as members of our wider military community, most of whom had no idea that Paul, Ed and I had been with Mike when he died.

Given my emotional fragility, rather than try to speak coherently to the family there and then, I vowed to write to his mother to explain Mike's role within my team on the night he died, in the hope that it might offer some comfort. I wanted to give reassurance that he had been among friends, doing what he loved and was at the very top of his game. I also wanted to share that Mike had been in a very good mood and we'd all been laughing and joking throughout the day, right up until the mission started. Had I tried to do this verbally, after the acute stress and emotion of the funeral, I would have struggled to say what I needed to.

I also thought she should know that it was Mike's personal contribution that led us to the target (which ended up being internationally significant), and, for that, she should be justifiably proud. While none of this would bring him back, I had heard from other widows and orphans of conflict that one of the biggest worries preventing closure can be a lack of detail about the events in question, combined with a dread that their loved one died alone or that they were unhappy in the hours or days leading up to their death. This was certainly not the case here and the contextualisation of key components helped us all make sense of this difficult and traumatic incident: a sense of a higher purpose, of things going well, of pride and of connection with others.

At home, the tempo was very different from the pace I'd got used to on operations. The next few weeks were boring but important, as I got into the routine of daily rehab and regular medical check-ups.

On one of my early medical consultations, I was desperate for the doctor to tell me the earliest date that I might be allowed to head back overseas. He said, of course, that it would be very much dependent on how my wounds healed and how well the rehab went. I pressed him harder. 'Six weeks' was the best he could offer, which felt like a lifetime away. I jokingly asked if we could negotiate . . . 'Four [weeks] for cash?!', which elicited a largely fair response of 'WHAT IS WRONG WITH YOU PEOPLE?!'

Ed, who'd been hit by shrapnel from one of the RPGs during the initial ambush, was recovering from an operation to remove metal embedded in his heel. Unfortunately, his injury had proved trickier than mine and he suffered continued aggravation and pain for years afterwards, which meant that he was not able to redeploy for that rotation. Like me, he was bored and frustrated by the enforced rest, so we tried to find ways to stay occupied, not least because we were acutely aware that cutting ourselves off from others as we dealt with our loss could be unhelpful – social connection is good for resilience, at the level of our very DNA.

On one of our free days after physio, we decided to drive up to

Selly Oak Hospital to see Paul, who'd been admitted as an inpatient while doctors worked on fixing his vision. As well as damage to his eye, he'd been hit with shrapnel in the elbow, but this was now healing well, leaving the loss of the lens as the priority.

We located the ophthalmic ward, which seemed to be populated predominantly by geriatrics waiting for, or recovering from, cataract operations. Luckily for Paul, following the discharge of another patient, he'd been given his own private room. However, as both Ed and I had been finding, too much time on your own was not necessarily a good thing.

Paul complained about being bored and told us that he spent most of the time staring out of the window onto the street several storeys below. We did our best to cheer him up and spent several hours making fun of each other and catching up on operational news. As visiting hours came to an end, we promised to stay in touch and, if he was likely to be stuck there for much longer, we would come back to see him the following week.

On our way out, trying not to slip with our crutches on the highly polished floor of the hospital corridor, we bumped into one of the hospital chaplains who stopped to ask what had happened to us.

We explained that we'd both been discharged after our own operations and had been visiting a colleague. The chaplain then asked how our friend was coping and if he needed any spiritual support. With a mischievous exchange of glances with Ed, I said that we *were*, in fact, a little worried about Paul, as he'd said how lonely he was and just wanted someone to talk to. The chaplain kindly agreed to check in on him regularly and bade us farewell.

Back at home, I focused on recovering my strength and fitness, as my left leg had lost a lot of muscle from being immobilised.

I was very keen to get signed off by the doctor as being fit. I needed a green light to redeploy. With some enduring discomfort, I adopted my best poker face and tried not to grimace through the final fitness test, which included requiring me to hop repeatedly on each leg.

The journey to this point had not been entirely straightforward.

Although I'd only been unable to bend my left leg for a few weeks, I was shocked to see how quickly it had weakened. Being forced to bend and stress my quads, while also having an evil physiotherapist manually break down the rapidly building scar tissue above my knee daily, felt like I was being electrocuted.

The fitness test resulted in a borderline pass, but the doctor gave me the benefit of the doubt and agreed to release me back into the wild. He did so, however, with caveats, insisting that I must continue to get daily physio once back in theatre and that I was to report to him if I felt at any stage that my injuries were preventing me from fully carrying out my role. In other words, at no time should I do anything that meant others might not be able to rely on me, thereby putting a mission at risk. Of course, I agreed, as this was non-negotiable, before starting to look for flight options.

Unfortunately, Ed and Paul's injuries had not healed as quickly, so I'd be going back without them, but we agreed to catch up before I left. It was during this catch-up that Paul told us what a nightmare the rest of his time at Selly Oak had been. He told us about a hospital chaplain who did not leave him alone, which had driven him to distraction. When we admitted the part we'd played his anger soon switched to grudging respect, once he admitted he would have done the same.

Although the major metalwork had been removed in those first few weeks, other smaller pieces of embedded shrapnel took longer to work their way to the surface of my arms and legs. Over a year later, the final piece had moved to a point just below the surface on the back of my thigh and was starting to irritate me. I tried to leave it alone but the more I touched it, the more I was convinced it was about to pop out. When it didn't, I decided that I could probably help it along. Stupidly, this idea came to me after a night out.

As I thought it would need only a small incision to be able to tease out the small piece of offending shrapnel, I believed I could do this minor surgery myself at home. After selecting the sharpest knife in the kitchen (which wasn't very), I heated the blade on the gas hob and then poured a little neat vodka over the end to sterilise it. I know. Idiot.

Sitting on the kitchen floor, I went to work. The first shock was how much it hurt. Without anaesthetic – I now accept that beer and vodka are not an equitable substitute – my amateur surgery stung like hell. Wincing, and with more blood than I was anticipating dripping onto the white tiled floor, I removed the shrapnel, which turned out to be much smaller than it felt.

Pleased with my handiwork, I went in search of antiseptic pads and a bandage.

The following morning, while nursing a hangover, it was evident that my efforts had not been as professional as I'd thought, with the wound continuing to leak. Admitting defeat, I drove into work so a doctor could grade my proficiency.

He was not impressed. To teach me a lesson, he declined to offer local anaesthetic and, a few stitches later, read me the riot act, and rightly so. Luckily, I hadn't done any long-term damage.

What is clear now, as I write this, is that I have no recollection of anyone asking me in any detail about how I was feeling or coping emotionally after these early traumas. Everything had been focused on the physical. Or perhaps somebody did and I have just forgotten, but the fact that I have so little memory of it makes me wonder how much focus there was on mental health back then. Regardless – thankfully in my case – I was able to process this and other experiences (several of which also took place on subsequent Halloweens) and, rather than dwelling on the negatives or being consumed with survivor's guilt, I concentrated on trying to ensure that Mike's loss, and the others that followed, was not in vain.

Although I'd never been aware of the term post-traumatic growth for much of my military career, I now realise that I was a living embodiment of it, as I'd manifested the first of five categories of growth, namely seeking and embracing new opportunities, as a child and in adulthood. Largely subconsciously at the time, I also now recognise I was developing a connection with all the other categories: building resilience and cultivating inner strength, forging closer relationships with those one loves and cares about, and finding joy in and being grateful for even the most simple things in life.

I realise that I am fortunate to be able to reflect on my own resilience, something that doesn't come easily to everybody. That said, life can sometimes throw us such a curveball that our once most innate skilfulness can still desert us, requiring us to actively engage in thinking our way to better resilience. The more we practise some of the techniques mentioned, the more likely we are to hardwire them into our minds, so they are more readily available to us when we really need them.

This does take commitment, but neuroscience assures us that with much mental practice, we can actually restructure our brains to become more resilient. So that's got to be worth some effort.

PRACTICAL TECHNIQUE: 'THE GOOD, THE BAD AND THE BORING'

The impact of dealing with trauma exposure is often not pretty. It is no wonder that the human brain struggles to put things down that are dangerous or abhorrent: it wants to protect us, to keep us vigilant to future harm. However, incidents – no matter how traumatic we may have found them – are made up of many components, including those that are positive, neutral or plain dull. Brains need this whole picture to file things away. We can help the brain by building this whole picture; seeing things from different spatial perspectives and putting them in different timescales (drawing maps from different angles, rewinding and fast-forwarding what happened). We can also add in extra information to neutralise the harmful parts of a memory, such as acts of professionalism, of care or respect, the routines and processes at play and even traces of the humorous or light-hearted. This bigger picture shrinks the traumatic material in the mind's eye and completes the memory.

Science and Thinking

Transitioning from traumatic experience to home

Transition from the combat theatre to home can be a very challenging time, as frames of reference shift from the harshness and visceral dynamic of the theatre to that of 'home', of routine and the banal. In the early 2010s, there was much research undertaken by the King's Centre for Military Health Research (Hunt et al., 2014) on how soldiers adjust to this mentally. Reservists came off worse in terms of PTSD, seemingly because they didn't have the chance to make sense of their experience in the company of others, as the regular serving soldiers did (who had access to Third Location Decompression). To read more, visit: https://kcmhr.org/.

Releasing tension

For more about how bodies retain the tension of our life experiences, a highly valuable read is The Body Keeps the Score by Bessel Van der Kolk (2014). There are many ways in which the body naturally stores tension and many ways to relieve that tension, the critical factor is to get to know one's own body to see where we naturally hold different types of tension and then what to do with it once we have tapped into it. A simple practical step is to introduce into your day a couple of moments to check in with our bodies and ask ourselves: are my shoulders raised or tight? Is my breathing shallow and rushed? Does my stomach feel tense or knotted? Are my eyes feeling prickly? We can use feeling anxious or stressed as a flag to us that we need to check in, or we can set reminders on our phone twice a day, or stick a note on an object we regularly reach for. Once we have tapped into the tension, closing our eyes for a few seconds, taking a deep exhale and then consciously loosening those body parts can do wonders as a mini reset for our body and brain, so we can refocus on what is important to us – and perhaps address more pragmatically what is generating the tension. Other approaches are to use apps which can talk us through releasing tension, such as sleep apps or those which offer a body scan.

The importance of social connection

It's very easy when we are in pain to contract around our suffering and cut ourselves off from others as we try to get on with it. This isn't helpful. Beyond scientific logic (Kohrt et al., 2020), we have accessible cognitive practices we can learn to help cultivate less isolation when we are struggling with something. As mentioned before, being able to recognise that there are others around us (or even far away from us, somewhere we can't see them) who may right now be experiencing what we are, or who maybe have messed up recently like we have, or have thought things that we may have, can be extremely centring. We have a tendency to assume that when we are struggling, our struggles are unique, cultivated out of unique us-shaped circumstances and influences. The truth is that we share so much as a species in so far as what we are affected by and how we react. A practical technique we can use when we are feeling very entwined in our own existence and isolated from everyone else is to select a person with one trait, possession, behaviour or thought similar to one of your own and, for a brief second, just say to oneself, 'Just like me'. This 'Just like me' technique has been developed by psychologist Jack Cornfield.

8

Constant Learning

Humility, Curiosity and Perspective: Powerful Predictors of Resilience

'Learning is a treasure that will follow its owner everywhere.'

Chinese proverb

Although I have never considered myself remotely academic, and despite being a disruptive pupil for several of my teenage years, I have always loved learning. Taking the opportunity to master a new skill, try a new sport, study a new language or embrace a new culture has been an approach I have applied throughout my life and have never regretted it. Even when the experience has led to an unanticipated or less positive outcome, I have always, without fail, learned something valuable. Not by thinking about what failure *might* teach me, but actually learning *through* failure. Or as Leonard Cohen opined in one of his songs, cracks are needed in everything, if light is to get in. Therefore, I believe that cracks are things to be valued and cherished, not hidden, as *kintsugi* artisans of Japan do when repairing damaged pottery.

For me, learning is something that can change us, rather than it being solely some kind of obligation to retain new information. Neuroscience backs this up (thank goodness!). Our brains are genuinely tuned in to what they can get from learning, beyond fulfilling a requirement or marking off an achievement. The real gem of this is that it has been shown there's a link to the sense of reward we get from learning (a spike in dopamine) to the functionality of a key area of the brain that makes sense of our world and protects us from trauma impact: the hippocampus. This means that we are wired to take pleasure in learning and this can also protect us from harm.

That said, we can only learn if we accept that we don't already know everything we need to know, and that is where humility comes into play. A combination of humility and curiosity is a powerful predictor of resilience. Neuropsychologically, new pathways are laid down more fully when there is a recognition that the new activity or understanding is valuable to us – we can't appreciate the value of corrected thinking if we don't acknowledge that the original thinking wasn't quite right in the first place.

I remain, therefore, a vociferous advocate of the belief that we are never too old to learn, particularly if it forces us out of our comfort zone and helps us to retain our hippocampal plasticity, the heart of the memory system, which neuroscience shows us we can train to change the way we think. As this is also the part of the brain that is vulnerable to age-related atrophy and early onset dementia, by learning to use it more, we can grow it, building its resilience to ageing.

Although work often gets in the way, I believe that it's important to take every opportunity to experience new things. Even if we try something only once, it often brings a fresh perspective and understanding, two things that are critical in healthy personal and professional lives as leaders, followers, partners and teammates.

Perspective, in particular, is crucial to the human brain; beyond giving us a sense of solidarity and connectedness, being aware of other perspectives allows our brains to settle as it reduces the perceived magnitude of what may have been causing us stress at the time (which is arguably one reason why we, as humans, love a good view).

It was not particularly out of character, therefore, that during my basic officer training at the Royal Military Academy, Sandhurst, I opted for a path less travelled and jumped with both feet into a completely new world. After being advised that I would be unlikely to secure one of only three places to join the Gurkhas that year, I decided to go for it anyway and was keen to prove the doubters wrong. Thankfully, my gamble paid off. On commissioning, I was posted to the 1st Battalion, Royal Gurkha Rifles, a constituent unit of the then 5th (Airborne) Brigade. As such, we were airborne light infantry and jungle warfare specialists which, in and of itself, presented some fascinating opportunities. My abiding memory of those early years was that this was a simple time, one of learning, adventure and growth, the first hurdle of which to clear was learning Nepali from scratch.

Although the working language of the British Army will always be English, as a Gurkha officer it was important to become as proficient a Nepali speaker as possible. To have failed in that aim would have meant that I'd have struggled to connect with my soldiers and would have missed important conversations, so I worked hard to ensure I could hold my own in most situations. Moreover, if we ever found ourselves in combat, it was likely that my soldiers would have reverted to their native tongue, given the way the brain's language centre behaves when under acute pressure.

With Gurkhas stationed at the time in the UK, Hong Kong and Brunei, there were abundant opportunities to thrive. There were also unexpected responsibilities, including the chance to carry out public duties in London. For a Guardsman of the Household Division, public duties constitute a core element of their peacetime role, so this would not generally be considered special. For Gurkhas, however, the opportunity to guard Buckingham Palace, St James's Palace or the Tower of London, came around infrequently and were a novel and exciting experience for the battalion.

During my own company's rotation, I found myself, as a 2nd Lieutenant, the most junior commissioned rank in the British Army, with responsibility for the Crown Jewels as Guard Commander of the Tower of London.

Unbeknown to me in advance, the Guard Commander was allocated a small apartment in one of the towers, within which was a large, red old-fashioned alarm bell emblazoned with 'JEWEL HOUSE ALARM' in supersized font. As part of my handover with the outgoing commander, I was handed a ring binder several inches thick, which contained instructions detailing what precisely I was required to do if the alarm sounded (something one expected to happen extremely rarely, if ever). I didn't make much of a dent in it before I was distracted by other matters but, thankfully, the alarm remained silent for the duration of my 24-hour stay.

No sooner had our public duties task ended than my unit's focus switched rapidly to preparing for a deployment to the Balkans; my first operational tour, and one that would leave a lasting impression on me.

Although I didn't join with any plans to leave the Gurkhas, as my exposure to other parts of the military grew the more I was keen to explore additional roles that were available only outside of our small regimental family. To that end, and after completing several incredible years in my battalion, I applied to see if I had what it takes to become a helicopter pilot.

I was very lucky to have an understanding regimental adjutant who, unlike some I'd heard about in other regiments, encouraged his soldiers to fly the nest. Some saw the loss of their own as something to be prevented or restricted. In my case, the battalion's leadership viewed opportunities such as this as chances for individual officer or soldier professional development and to showcase the Gurkhas to the rest of the army. To that end, there was always a healthy slew of Gurkhas to be found in all four corners of the world.

After passing the initial pilot medical and written application, I was loaded onto the next available pilots' grading course, an intensive package of light aircraft lessons designed to assess aptitude; a necessary step prior to being selected for helicopter training. Although I had never flown a plane at this point, I hoped that some aviation genes might have been passed down to me from my maternal grandfather Eddie, who had been a navigator in the RAF. Leafing through his flying logbook after he died, it became clear that not only had he served throughout the Second World War, but that he'd flown in almost every type of bomber in service in Europe, Africa and the Far East, concluding his career on the Avro Lancaster with 617 'Dambusters' Squadron after Operation Chastise. His service record and his humility inspired me hugely.

Throughout grading we flew several times a day, with each lesson becoming more challenging and advanced.

During one sortie, just as I was gaining confidence, my instructor – a retired RAF officer with thousands of hours under his belt – announced that it was 'time to try a loop'. I watched him complete the manoeuvre before he handed me the controls.

It started well, with the small two-seater Firefly 160 diving and picking up speed, before I pulled back the stick to take us into a steep climb. I'm not entirely sure what happened next except that, whatever I did, it didn't feel right. As the plane lost speed and dribbled to a stop at the top of the loop we became fully inverted before the plane stalled violently and began to spin.

With the situation appearing, at least from my side of the cockpit, to be deteriorating rapidly, my instructor did nothing.

I battled unsuccessfully to regain control.

We had not covered this eventuality in the pre-flight briefing and I had no idea what to do. Unable to look with any clarity at the outside world, which was now flashing green-blue green-blue, earth-sky, earth-sky, I tried to focus instead on the cockpit instruments to see if I could work out what the hell was going on. With G-forces increasing, we hung precariously from our harnesses, swinging like bats from side to side due to the nauseating oscillation, as the plane sought to return us to the airfield, with or without my assistance.

The artificial horizon – one of the most important instruments in the cockpit, indicating the orientation of the aircraft relative to the earth's horizon outside – provided me with few clues, while the plane rotated seemingly randomly around it, so I fixed my gaze instead on the altimeter, which was even more terrifying. It appeared to be winding down at an alarming rate (just like in the movies, shortly before the pilot usually ejects), and with the accelerometer needle going in the opposite direction, I began to feel very light-headed. Rather than using the pedals to recover from the spin (which I later learned was the correct thing to do), I had instead used the stick, which served only to increase the violence and speed of movement.

After what felt like an eternity, and with me having failed to do anything helpful to correct my initial rookie pilot mistake, my instructor's voice drifted calmly over the intercom: 'I have control now.'

Almost instantly, we flipped back the right way up and normal flight resumed. When I asked why it had taken him so long to intervene, he said he'd been keen to see if I would know instinctively what to do. It was patently clear that I did not!

Despite the unsettling Maverick and Goose inverted spin mishap, we survived, and I graded well enough to be allocated a slot on the full Joint Army Pilots' Course. This was not without its stresses, especially as I have never been a whizz mathematician. Having read that it's commonly accepted one should be good at maths to be a competent pilot, I had to work hard to keep up with the technical lessons about principles of flight, aircraft systems, how to calculate the coefficient of lift and other such perplexing (to me at least) equations. But with a dogged determination to improve, in the end I relished being forced out of my comfort zone and made more than a little vulnerable, as the reward of succeeding and becoming a pilot was worth it.

Once we were through the classroom theory, the hard work really began. The requirement to keep pace with the curriculum was relentless. Every flying lesson saw us loaded up with new skills we were expected to master or face 'the chop' – being cut from the course and returned to parent regiments, tail between legs.

For anyone who has struggled learning to drive, imagine being let loose on the road without your instructor after only a few lessons. This was no different. While the prospect of being sent off to fly solo after only six- or seven-hours' experience was exhilarating, if I am honest, it also seemed a little foolhardy.

No time to worry about that now. It was my turn. Help!

With the sun shining and only the slightest hint of a breeze on the airfield, I found myself in the first batch of students to be sent up. While our instructors would not have let us go if they didn't think we could complete the sortie safely, as I taxied alone to line up on the runway threshold for final pre-flight checks, I suddenly had flashbacks to my inverted stall/spin incident and became very aware that the seat next to me was empty. Not to worry; I just pretended it wasn't and talked through all the procedures and checks, exactly as I would have done if my instructor was there.

I've learned that a good way of dealing with doubt or fear (which may be accompanied by intrusive thoughts) is to have in the memory bank a time when we've had a similar experience that turned out positively (using Rick Hanson's HEAL technique again), which, in my case, was every other flight I'd completed in the preceding few weeks. Another tip for those of us who experience subtle intrusions (unbidden thoughts) or more full-on flashbacks, is to simply acknowledge them as that (an intrusion in your day) out loud, to bring you back to the present. This may give our brains just enough momentary awareness for us to decide what to 'do' in response to the flashback.

The initial solo was designed to be simple, with students required only to fly a couple of circuits around the airfield, but that didn't make the experience any less nerve-wracking.

Thankfully, and clearly deliberately, the Firefly is a forgiving aircraft, so even when my landings were occasionally bumpy (which one of my instructors rudely referred to as 'arrivals'), there was not too much we could do to mess things up. Even though, deep down, we all willed everyone to do well, the abuse we would give and receive if we performed anything other than a perfect landing was harsh.

Calling 'Short finals' over the radio (the call one makes to air traffic control to confirm your intent to land), my eyes were drawn to the gaggle of course mates standing in line on the left-hand side of the runway next to our crew room. It was only after I touched down, with a couple of nervous bounces, that I saw they were holding up large, numbered score cards, rather like judges on *Strictly Come Dancing*. With only the lowest of scores – ones and twos – being raised you knew you must have done OK.

While our elementary flying training took place at RAF Barkston Heath in Lincolnshire, different phases of this 18-month-long course saw us travel to many parts of the UK. Basic helicopter training was conducted at RAF Shawbury in Shropshire, specialist mountain flying in Snowdonia National Park, Wales, with advanced tactical training and conversion to the Lynx Mk.7 multi-role helicopter taking place in Middle Wallop, Hampshire, not far from where I grew up.

Apart from the constant worry that a few bad flights could start the downward spiral that might lead to getting chopped, flying training and the operational deployment that followed were periods of constant learning, incredible camaraderie and a lot of fun. And with the commitment I made to myself at school, to never turn down the chance to try something new (unless patently dangerous or illegal . . .), the opportunities for adventure just kept on coming.

It had become my default state of mind or raison d'être; something I have continued through the rest of my life.

Even during the Covid-19 pandemic I struggled to sit idle, seeking ways to operate within the rules and expand my horizons.

Trying freediving for the first time, learning to paramotor and running my first ultra-marathon (albeit in the hotel room) were certainly not activities I anticipated would be on offer at the start of that difficult period. But each time I do this and learn a new skill or take up a new hobby I always meet incredible people and make a slew of wonderful new friends in the process, and I love it.

Beyond the more traditional learning, however, where one might pick up skills that result in a certificate or badge, some of the most important lessons for me have been about relationships, both personal and professional.

Adopting a growth mindset and being actively open to new ideas as well as trying to be more self-aware can be game-changing for how we approach every aspect of our lives. Consciously making time to understand how different experiences and perspectives shape our thinking and behaviour is time never wasted. We've already discussed the fact that in neuropsychology shifting perspectives and extending perspectives can boost the hippocampal processing of difficult experiences and help us regulate our stress response. But we can apply this to people, too. We can all be better partners, employees, leaders and teammates, but unless we recognise, honestly, our own strengths and weaknesses, we will not improve. We are all products of our individual upbringing, culture, religion and experiences, each of us viewing the world through a unique lens.

In my own life, two of the most impactful learnings have been on a more human, emotional level.

I now realise that I held for many years, albeit subconsciously, several biases and a binary view, not least with respect to relationships. Whether this was because of, directly or indirectly, my own early experiences as a child I'm not sure. Either way, as I look back at the period when the friends who had got married young began to divorce, I (then unmarried) often passed silent judgement. Of course, I had no idea what had led to their break-ups or who might be to blame, but, for reasons I can neither remember nor justify, I held an entirely unreasonable, superior view, telling myself that I would not ever let something like that happen to me.

It was a hell of a shock, therefore, when my own marriage unravelled with alarming speed a few years later. It was then that I realised I had no right to judge others, as I had clearly done, a realisation that filled me with both guilt and embarrassment.

I had learned a valuable lesson in humility and empathy for others – about not leaping to judgement, particularly when I knew none of the facts and had not walked in any of their shoes.

Having spent more than two decades in uniform, exposed to a variety of situations involving trauma, I felt confident that I knew and understood what kinds of incidents might cause or trigger post-traumatic stress. How wrong I was. Meeting military veterans, as well as Afghan refugees fleeing persecution by the Taliban, each with a very different experience and scarred by a variety of traumatic events, has given me a much-needed opportunity to reframe my thinking.

In his books, including *Sapiens* and *Homo Deus*, intellectual historian Yuval Noah Harari argues that our evolution as a species is critically dependent on our ability to learn from each other's experiences. It's perhaps no wonder that I've felt that dopamine spike when I've had that opportunity on my own travels.

Taking time to listen and learn from those who've had the courage to seek help, and have picked themselves up and are now on a growth path, has been one of the most rewarding aspects of my life and one that I treasure. Understanding how others have managed to keep going, build resilience and overcome their own adversity, despite the mental and physical wounds they carry, continues to inspire me every day.

PRACTICAL TECHNIQUE: 'BEGINNER'S MIND'

In this chapter we have explored how learning can keep us young, fresh and adaptive to what is coming next. Yet, when we are faced with difficult circumstances it is not always easy to fess up to our ignorance. We learned earlier that acknowledging 'not knowing' can be a very skilful tool for resilience. When we accept what we don't know, we are actually more open to improving our experience and growing, as we take in fresh information and have new ideas as to how to respond to particular situations. This is much more lucrative than closing our mind down because we think we already know best.

Science and Thinking

Language centres of the brain and stress

Did you ever feel the inability to speak when you were nervous as a child? (Usually accompanied by the obligatory question, 'What, has the cat got your tongue?' from the nearest unsympathetic adult.) Do you find that when you start to verbalise something that has been playing on your mind, you can slowly start to feel a release of tension in your body and your breathing gets deeper? These are your language centres doing their thing. They go quiet when we're stressed (because evolution shows us that, when it comes down to it, if we are under threat, we need to act, not chat) and the same language centres wake up to help us connect to others and not to feel so alone after the immediate threat has gone (Guha et al., 2020).

Humility

Humility is seen in the field of occupational psychology as a learnable leadership skill (Zhu et al., 2019). It is worth considering that the feeling of shame is, for want of a better phrase the 'ugly sister' of humility. Shame is something that many of us may have learned to live with – when coming from a childhood drenched in adversity, for example – but if that habit continues as we mature, this can be bad news for recovering from trauma in later life (Fine et al., 2023). The difference between humility and shame is key to resilience: showing humility earns the trust and respect from those whom we are leading, whereas shame prevents us from leading ourselves towards our goals and sometimes the help we very much need.

Dealing with intrusions

Visual or audio intrusions are also referred to as flashbacks or hearing things or voices. In popular culture they are a trademark symptom of PTSD, but they aren't confined to those who have clinical levels of trauma impact. There are many techniques out there on how to cope with intrusions; learning what works for you is your choice and your right. Ironing out a traumatic memory in space and time by applying mapping and timeline techniques (previously mentioned in relation to trauma memory) may help to reinsert the intrusion into the proper context from which it originates (Miller et al., 2020 and Miller, 2022). Further therapeutic work such as Eye Movement Desensitisation and

Reprogramming (EMDR) is also worth considering, as is good old talking therapy which may be readily available through your GP. The British Association for Counselling and Psychotherapy offers a good explanation of EMDR.

9

Resilience under Pressure

Avoiding Hijack and Remembering the Vital Nature of Self-Care

> 'You can measure a man's character by the choices he makes under pressure.'
>
> Winston Churchill, British prime minister (1940–5 and 1951–5)

In my own research, I found multiple definitions of resilience as being about the ability to adapt successfully in the face of stress and adversity. While this goes some way to capturing the essence of what I think resilience means in principle, it lacks, in my opinion, a critical word: 'learn'. It is important, of course, to be able to adapt in the moment when faced with something unfamiliar, uncertain or scary – a skill in its own right – but if we do not *learn* from each experience, we risk repeating the mistakes we will invariably make.

If the above definition of resilience is altered slightly so that it becomes: 'the ability to adapt *and learn* in the face of stress and adversity', then I've been lucky, or unlucky, to have had plenty of practice. And with definitions of adversity including terms such as 'hardship, misfortune, distress, suffering and unhappiness', being able to move quickly beyond situations that involve these feelings or outcomes, in good mental or physical shape, is key to developing and improving resilience.

But how much resilience are we born with and how much do we need to navigate and overcome life's challenges?

Frustratingly, it's not until you find yourself in the arena for the first time, as Theodore Roosevelt once said, with a face 'marred by dust and sweat and blood', that you know for sure if you have what it takes to handle the pressure and prevail. A bit late for many of us!

Now, the good news is that resilience, like leadership, can be taught, learned and developed, so any one failure does not define or determine future outcomes, something to which I can attest both as a child and as an adult. However, in that teaching we must acknowledge our body's sensory response to our environment. Resilience might be fundamentally a cognitive skill, but it needs to tune into the messages bombarding the body. The feel of an experience must be acknowledged before it can be put down and the understanding of an experience can take over. Training ourselves in basic body awareness and grounding is a good way to start.

Case in point: my first big gun battle saw me, in my own mind at least, come up short. Everything happened so fast. It was unexpected, unfamiliar and frightening.

However, despite lingering irritation with my own performance in the arena on that fateful night, the lessons I learned on the back of it and the resilience I built in the weeks, months and years that followed, set me up to be a better commander later in my career, when faced with more complex leadership challenges. So, as hard as it was, I am grateful for that early failure and what it taught me personally about leadership, although, unsurprisingly, the loss of a colleague in that first wave of machine-gun fire is something from which none of us who were there will ever fully recover. It could have been any one of us. It probably should have been more than one of us.

Given that no two incidents are ever the same, being able to first adapt – to dynamically changing, unpredictable situations – and then learn from that adaptation and how it affected the outcome, is critical, whether in a personal or professional context. Achieving one without the other – adapting without learning – may therefore not be enough.

Our willingness or ability to embrace complexity and identify opportunities that can exist in uncertain situations, rather than seeing primarily risk and threat, significantly increases our ability to overcome challenges of every kind. Harnessing a sense of fluidity and open-mindedness enables us to be far more flexible in our response.

When we are in 'threat response' mode, typically our mind will contract around what we know and don't know in order for us to respond quickly and effectively. When we are repeatedly faced with immediate threats (be it in our professional life or through difficult personal circumstances) our brains become very used to contracting around the black and white, the binary of yes and no, of danger or safety. This mentality can very gradually creep into other arenas of our thinking and our lives, unless we deliberately practice exploring different perspectives and ideas when we are not under stress.

This independence of habitual thinking is known to be important for resilience and our happiness: when we default to seeing things in very concrete ways, involving judgement, comparing or planning and we don't open up to imagination, creativity, alternative options and mindsets, it can lead to dullness and even depression. Flexibility in choosing how we think about things is the ultimate key to resilience and, as I can confirm, it is extremely liberating and empowering.

My instinct on my first difficult Halloween was to see primarily risk – very real, life-threatening risk – combined with a failure to anticipate how that risk might manifest. But with more time and experience under my belt, I got better at accepting and expecting the need to adapt and stopped fearing the uncertainty and unpredictability that accompanies all things complex.

Instead, I began to take advantage of the often-incredible freedom this brought to shape outcomes more in my favour.

With time, the cumulative nature of my own trauma and the compound learning that has come from tackling it head-on has contributed significantly to how resilient I have become. This often requires direct acknowledgement of what didn't go well and what could have been different. I have learned that facing these honest insights is almost like picking up precious tools to make me stronger next time round. The sense of failure begins to sting less, soothed with the balm of what could be possible in the future because of this new learning. A brain that is thirsty to learn is often more eager to forgive too.

Consciously taking positive lessons from each event, I now think of resilience as a currency. By crediting my resilience bank account whenever I get through something hard and learn from it, I've been able to build up a working balance from which I can draw, giving me the courage and confidence to face my fears when I need to.

One such incident saw my team tested to the limit, forcing each member (to extend the metaphor) to make withdrawals from, in some cases, dwindling funds.

The coalition unit to which I was attached as a liaison officer had been tasked with detaining a notorious terrorist. Intelligence indicated that he was hiding in an isolated farmhouse a short helicopter ride from their forward operating base. A pager alert directed us to get to the team room as fast as we could, a short distance from the helicopters that would take us to our destination.

After a quick mission brief, we boarded the helicopters and launched towards the target, hoping to secure a straightforward detention, ideally without a fight. If all went smoothly, we would be back at base within 60 to 90 minutes. However, recent experience told us that conducting a high-profile operation, in broad daylight and in an area known colloquially as the 'Triangle of Death', remained a high-risk activity.

And so it proved.

As the formation neared the drop-off point near a large farm complex, we began taking fire. Our two supporting helicopter gunships returned the favour, striking a minivan into which several insurgents had jumped as they attempted to flee. Hitting a stash of rockets and explosives hidden in the back, the van exploded, sending an acrid plume of black smoke high into hazy sky.

It was becoming clear that the insurgents had no intention of coming quietly and we began to wonder if we had brought enough water and food for a protracted fight in scorching summer temperatures. (Note to self: remembering to cover the basics of self-care is important in normal life; something that is even more vital when under acute stress or threat. Neglecting our basic needs in these circumstances can be catastrophic.)

As my team debussed into an unexpectedly boggy, ploughed field, running for cover was a significantly slower and stickier affair than any of us anticipated, while the gun battle between the helicopters and insurgents raged above us.

Due to the intensity of the fire from the farmhouse, the commander called in an air strike.

With smoke still billowing from the minivan, coalition jets dropped two laser-guided bombs directly onto the main building, while we hunkered down in a shallow trench around one hundred yards away across the open field.

Waiting for a missile of any size to impact close to you makes for an uneasy time. Although I didn't spot either of the bombs until a fraction of a second before they struck, I certainly heard them. Their arrival was foreshadowed by a chilling whistling sound as they passed through the last few hundred feet before detonating. As the dust settled, following the double impact and blast waves that accompanied them, we were shocked to see a group of women and children exit one of the adjacent buildings, waving their hands. As they approached, we saw that some had sustained minor wounds from the blast. Ushering them towards the nearest assault team, a few fighters who'd also survived the explosions continued to harass the helicopters circling overhead.

In line with the international law of armed conflict, it was our duty to ensure that the wounded were given appropriate medical treatment. To that end, we recalled one of our insertion helicopters to extract and escort the group of injured civilians to a military hospital.

What happened next, however, was baffling.

Despite knowing very well that their family members were now on board, enemy fighters tried frantically to shoot down the helicopter as it departed, thankfully resulting only in superficial bullet damage to the fuselage. The logic of this, and other similar incidents I witnessed on other operations, where fighters deliberately killed or put at risk their own families, was something I never understood. I made a mental note never to allow myself to forget it.

Once the helicopter containing the women and children was clear, we got back to the task at hand: moving tactically towards the farmhouse to detain the remaining insurgents or neutralise the threat they posed.

With heavy and persistent firing continuing, the gunship pilots reported 'Winchester', meaning they'd already expended all their ammunition. However, because the pilots were 'soldiers first', they continued to fly passes over the target, using personal weapons to provide at least some covering fire while we waited for other assets to arrive, as to have left us completely exposed would have given the enemy an unhelpful advantage. Given the lack of intimate gunship support, the ground commander requested for the sleeping night crews back at base to be alerted in case things deteriorated further.

Movement across the ploughed field continued to be slow going as we made our way to link up with the lead element of our team.

Another burst of heavy weapon fire punctured the temporary calm provided by my noise-cancelling headphones, which in turn was replaced by an angry metallic scream somewhere above me, which I can only liken to the sound of a machine in its death throes or at least in considerable distress.

My immediate concern was that another bomb was on its way in, which would have been both inconvenient and dangerous given that we were completely exposed.

As I tried to process this awful mechanical clattering filling my ears, which was getting more intense by the second, one of the gunships plopped unceremoniously into the mud just a few feet to our left. Unbeknown to either us or the crew at that moment, several of the rotor blades had sustained damage from a heavy calibre machine gun during their last pass over the target, hence the awful noise. For the pilot to be able to land such a badly damaged aircraft in relative control is testament to his exceptional skill and a very cool head under pressure.

Recognising that their airborne fire support role was over for now, the crew shut down, jumped out and asked where they could best support us. It was so refreshing to see that these guys were willing to adapt on the fly, focused as they were entirely on the mission, doing whatever was necessary for the greater good of the team. Quitting was just not in their nature.

Finally linking up with the group who'd secured the farmhouse, sensitive site exploitation began. This meant looking in detail at the vehicle containing the now exploded rockets, as well as searching for any other useful intelligence from inside or around the target that might tie the leader to the network within which he played a part.

While that process continued, we received the unwelcome news from one of the airborne surveillance aircraft that 'a truck with maybe thirty or forty fighters appears to be heading in your direction'. Although nobody panicked, despite the suggested size of this group outnumbering (and probably outgunning) us, we needed to think quickly and carefully about establishing a robust defensive position to hold our territory.

As we were a relatively small force, the challenge of facing an enemy two to three times our size was not insignificant. We were keen to keep them at arm's length, if possible, as close-quarter fighting could soon get untidy.

Following positive identification of the truck containing the fighters, another missile was requested, in an attempt to slow or thwart their approach. Enemy coordinates were passed by radio, together with our own location, and once the necessary approvals were given, the fast jet crew was authorised to drop.

Waiting for bombs to strike a hundred yards from you is one

thing, but the anticipation of munitions landing 'danger close' when you are without significant cover is quite another. My team was located on one side of a large earth berm, several feet high, making it impossible for us to see the target vehicle, or indeed most of our own colleagues. It was a disconcerting feeling being so blind but there was precious little we could do about it. This was a clear example of having to acknowledge and accept the alarm signals coming from our brains, which registered that the situation in which we found ourselves was uncomfortable, but then making the decision not to be hijacked or overwhelmed by it, as there was nothing much we could do about it. Not fighting the obvious discomfort allowed us to reserve our energy to concentrate on what might come next.

To that end, we paired up calmly, weapons at the ready, with spare ammunition laid out to enable rapid reloads should the insurgents suddenly break through our position and try to overwhelm us. We were ready to fight to the last man, or last bullet, if that's what it came to.

Once the clipped 'Missile away' message crackled over the radio, we lay down with faces pressed into the hot dirt.

The next few seconds felt like minutes, as the blazing afternoon sun beat down on our backs and salty sweat dripped irritatingly into my eyes, despite attempts to wipe it away. When the now-familiar whistling of the bomb's final seconds broke the silence, I tensed and held my breath, bracing for the explosion.

We were not disappointed.

As the missile detonated, far closer than I think any of us was expecting, the earth literally moved beneath us; a sensation akin to being on a small boat in a heavy swell.

As my brain struggled to compute what had just happened, we were showered with clods of scorching earth.

From the testimonies of those wounded in other conflicts, when razor-sharp, cauterising, shrapnel hits them, many cite having not felt it or having not realised the extent of the damage inflicted. I was a little concerned, therefore, that this might be the case for us, too. So, it was with considerable trepidation that we asked each other in turn to check that all our limbs were attached and if there was any obvious sign of bleeding, before having the confidence to look for ourselves.

Like the others, I had been covered from head to toe but because whatever had hit us was extremely hot, it was impossible to tell whether the warm feeling that persisted once the dust settled was purely soil, heated by the blast, or if we were bleeding. My partner assured me that he couldn't see any blood, so I picked myself up and shook off the remaining earth.

We couldn't work out why the blast had felt so close and why we'd been covered in so much detritus as we didn't think the enemy truck had been *that* near.

We later learned that, when coordinates had been passed to the fast jets, the grids had been misunderstood and the bomb had been dropped on us rather than the enemy vehicle. So, rather than missing the enemy, the bomb had only just missed *us*, exploding just the other side of the berm next to which we'd been lying. As is the case in most contact battles, things can get easily confused, something this bomb incident proved yet again. Although we had a few choice words we were very keen to share with the pilot, once we realised it was a classic 'fog of war' cock-up we let it go. In highly dynamic situations it can be very confusing and mistakes are made. Rather than seeking to apportion blame to any one person, we ultimately chose smart compassion.

With one helicopter down and the second returning to base to refuel, we remained exposed.

After what had just happened, the mission commander was reluctant to call in another air strike, so we waited for the night crews to join us while continuing to suppress the remaining enemy fighters in the truck attempting to reach our position.

When the next message we received ordered us to move at best speed to the 'crash site' and 'secure the downed bird', we were confused.

We replied that we were already at the site, assuming they were referring to the wounded aircraft that had nearly landed on us 30 minutes earlier. The message was sent again, this time stating that another bird would transport us about half a mile down the road.

Only then did we understand this meant that one of our night crews had been hit.

Given the complexity of the battle on the ground, the second pair of helicopters had been flying in a holding pattern just a few miles to the south, waiting to be called in once the initial air strikes had concluded. It was during one of these orbits that they'd been hit, potentially by the same heavy machine gun that brought down their sister aircraft.

With a sense of foreboding, our team of four made the short flight to the second crash site, which we located easily thanks to the tendrils of black smoke beginning to rise in the distance. I hoped and prayed during those few short minutes in transit that both pilots had managed to survive the impact and, just like the gunship crew brought down earlier near the farmhouse, that they too would be waiting for us, smiles on their faces, weapons at the ready, asking what we needed them to do.

To reduce the risk of becoming an obvious target ourselves, we flew just a few feet above the ground, putting down just a few hundred yards from the crash site.

Moving tactically but quickly, we navigated several boggy drainage ditches and low-level crops to reach a metalled road, running between us and the field in which the aircraft was burning. Dropping off two of our team to cover the road, I pushed forward with the team commander to check for survivors.

Given how few of us there were on the ground, we were isolated and extremely vulnerable.

Hearing continued reports of large numbers of fighters still roaming the area looking for trouble, we had to proceed with extreme caution. Yet, we wanted and needed to move quickly in case there was any chance of saving the crew.

With memories of the grainy 1993 news footage from operations in Somalia playing in my mind, which saw the body of a downed US army pilot dragged through the streets of Mogadishu by a baying mob, we had clear instructions that this kind of desecration would not be tolerated. We must defend the pilots, the aircraft and the site, at all costs.

Tragically, as we reached the impossibly twisted carcass of the aircraft, I could see the silhouettes of both pilots still strapped into their seats. They were already dead, but the team commander and I agreed that we had to do something, so we moved closer with the aim of cutting them free. However, this aircraft had been on its way to support our ground battle at the original target and was, therefore, fully loaded with ammunition. And, due to the intensity of the fire, this meant that the ammunition had begun 'cooking off' (that is to say it was exploding in the heat), causing bullets, rockets and other projectiles to fire randomly in all directions.

We wrestled to free the crew for several minutes, but it was proving to be an impossible task, due to the heat, flames and the fact that both pilots were wearing equipment that had jammed or snagged, trapping them in their seats.

With my own gloves now starting to burn and bullets zinging past us with increasing frequency, it was not a safe place to be. So it was with heavy hearts that we made the very difficult decision to withdraw, concluding that, as much as we wanted to remove and treat them with the utmost dignity, there was a very real chance that either or both of us would also be killed in the process, making an already tragic situation even worse. Thankfully, as we were able to discuss our options in the moment, and also leverage our professional experience, neither of us suffered moral injury as a result of the decisions we made.

As if to tell us that we had made the right decision, just as we began to withdraw several larger munitions duly exploded, engulfing what was left of the fuselage in an even more ferocious fireball.

Pulling back to our teammates by the road, the commander and I were deflated at having failed to cut the crew free. But rather than deter us, it filled each of us with a steely resolve to do whatever it took to prevent the enemy from desecrating their remains.

No sooner had we retaken our small defensive position than a white Toyota pickup appeared in the distance, inching erratically towards us. The fact that it was not driving at a normal speed and was veering from side to side seemed odd.

Through my scope I identified what appeared to be three adult males in the cab, so the commander and I fired several warning shots. Had the occupants merely been curious innocent civilians investigating the crash site, they would probably have stopped, turned around or quickly reversed and left. They did none of these. Instead, the vehicle faced us head-on and accelerated. As it did so, the front-seat passenger emptied an entire magazine of automatic fire through the windscreen. With little cover to speak of, other than a shallow depression we were already in, there were few (i.e. zero) good hiding options.

Having already used several of my nine lives by this point, not least during the Halloween ambush, miraculously, yet again, I got away with it. Neither I nor any member of the team was hit, despite the volume of fire directed at us.

With this escalation, we returned fire, disabling the vehicle approximately 50 yards from our position. There is nothing quite like being targeted by automatic fire to heighten the senses. But despite the adrenaline, heavy perspiration and elevated heart rates beating in our ears, once the vehicle stopped an eerie silence descended on the scene, as we watched and waited. And waited and watched.

I had been pretty sure that I'd seen three figures in the vehicle before the shooting started, two in the front and one in the back, so we continued to scan for any signs of life. Nothing needed to be said, as we were all focused solely on that vehicle and any further threat to life posed by any surviving occupants.

Although there was no discernible movement from the driver or his machine-gun-wielding passenger, after an hour or so I thought I spotted a flicker of activity in the back seat of the cab, but then nothing.

As we watched the surveillance aircraft circling above us, providing a degree of comfort that we were not entirely on our own, they kept us updated about what else was going on that we couldn't see, beyond our immediate vicinity.

Although helpful, their message that a truck with yet more armed men was heading in our direction was the last thing we needed to hear. But rather than being overwhelmed with fear, as perhaps we should have been, there was an air of calm and an acceptance that this was exactly the kind of situation for which we had been selected and trained. And rather than panic, we had a very matter-of-fact conversation about who would do what in a number of likely scenarios relating to any of us being wounded or killed.

In that moment I realised that I had become strangely comfortable with the very uncomfortable, and just thought logically about what I would do if I was the last member of the team, knowing that the colleagues and friends to my left and to my right would be doing the same.

We thought only about the mission and each other.

Without consciously stopping to think about it at the time, our calm and collected response to what was a crazy situation showed that we had all become, each in our own way, highly resilient; able to adapt and accept the uniquely stressful environments in which we chose to place ourselves. Fortunately, the truck never made it to our position, saving us from the need to put our 'fight to the last bullet' plan to the test.

After several more hours under the blistering sun, there was a sudden flurry of movement, followed by the back door of the truck flying open. Out leapt an adult male dressed in jeans and a T-shirt.

Having watched the truck for so long without seeing any visible movement, this came as quite a surprise.

When he jumped out, we sent several more warning shots in his direction, to deter him from trying to rush our position. Lifting his T-shirt, presumably to show us he was not wearing a suicide vest, he immediately dived back into the truck, forcing us to resume watching and waiting. Despite the actions of his friends earlier in the day, if he was unarmed he was not, at that moment, a legitimate target.

As our initial mission had been to conduct a quick detention at the farmhouse and return immediately to base, we had only the supplies for an operation that would ordinarily have been done and dusted in under two hours. By late afternoon, we were already very low on water and having to use our radios sparingly, to save batteries and avoid losing communications with those who would be organising our extraction or providing fast jet fire support, should we need it again.

With the sun beginning to break on the horizon, as the sounds of evening prayer floated across a light and mercifully slightly cooler early evening breeze, we had seen no further activity. Yet we remained convinced that there was still potential for something to happen, so we continued to watch the vehicle intently.

I began to wonder what the headquarters might be planning for the crashed aircraft, which had now burned itself out, when a message confirmed that the specialist Downed Aircraft Recovery Team (DART) would be arriving in a few hours to dismantle what was left and recover the crew. Understandably, they wanted to wait until dark so they could work with slightly less risk. But we really needed to know the exact status of the occupants of the vehicle in front of us to be sure that they were no longer a threat to us *or* the DART, who would be working close by.

We didn't have to wait long.

Shortly after night had fallen, there was another sudden whirlwind of activity as the same adult male leapt from the truck and started running towards us.

During his first exit, we had not positively identified any weapon but there was no mistaking his intent this time, as he loosed a long burst of automatic fire in our direction. With our infra-red lasers and night vision, he made for an obvious target.

Whether he self-detonated a suicide vest that he must have put on before jumping out of the vehicle for the second time, or one of our rounds hit it, remains unclear. Either way, there was a blinding flash, followed a split-second later by a big bang, and then silence.

Surveillance aircraft confirmed that they could not identify any additional heat sources, but to make sure that there was nothing else in the truck that would surprise us or the DART, we requested one final missile strike to destroy what remained of the vehicle.

Once the DART had completed their task with surgical efficiency, we called for a final extraction.

Loading the bodies of the crew into the back of our extraction helicopter and flying back to base was a trip I will never forget. Although it was not a particularly long flight, it gave us plenty of opportunity to reflect, yet again, on the impact and horrors of war. Although I didn't know either of the pilots personally, they were part of our wider military family and brotherhood. We all felt their loss as keenly as if they'd been close friends, not least because they were only there to support us and had paid with their lives.

On arrival at the military hospital, our team insisted on being the ones to escort the crew to the mortuary and, after completing the necessary paperwork, we left, subdued. It was only then, noticing that it was now well after midnight, I remembered it was my birthday. But there was nothing to celebrate.

After so many hours spent in the scorching sun, we were dangerously dehydrated, so we each guzzled pints of water when we got back to our accommodation, before trying to get some rest. However, sleep didn't come easily that night. This had been a marathon mission that had started out very differently from how it ended.

We were required to adapt to the complexity of the situation in which we found ourselves, all while under extreme pressure – environmental, physical and mental. The pressure had been prolonged and intense, but each of us had handled it well in our own way.

Perhaps the collective focus in our profession on training for the very worst eventualities helped, but I believe strongly that the resilience I had built in childhood contributed in some way to my overall tolerance of uncertainty and adversity, and my ability to move beyond the trauma or scars that those experiences left behind.

With the nature, scale and frequency of how each of us experiences trauma differing markedly, there is no template or formula to determine how each of us might be triggered or how we can overcome post-traumatic stress. But, taking every lesson from the most traumatic things we've faced (which for many will likely include extended Covid-19 isolation and concomitant stress and pressure) and depositing them in our bank account of resilience will better enable us to face future difficulties. That is not to say that we won't require novel solutions to new challenges, but knowing that we have done it before when the odds were stacked against us should certainly give us confidence that we can do it again.

PRACTICAL TECHNIQUE: 'STOP'

In this chapter we have explored what it is like to have to make difficult choices when our mind is being distracted and when we have forgotten our own strengths and needs. The simplest technique to remember in acute situations like this is to remember the acronym STOP: **S**top, **T**ake a breath, **O**bserve, **P**roceed. By following this, we instantaneously down-regulate our stress response and allow a little space to gather ourselves before we take action. It sounds ridiculously simple, but this is what we default to doing when we are in a chilled, regulated state. When we are stressed, we bypass this bit and wonder why things don't work out. The best physical stop is a natural *big breath out*. The mental stop will follow more easily once we do this.

Science and Thinking

The chemical basis of emotions

For some reason, Western society tends not to acknowledge the basic science that shows how emotions are actually sets of chemical instructions that are produced in response to environmental stimuli and guide us to action. Every emotion we can verbalise will emanate from a chemical reaction – and it is said in popular psychology that there isn't one emotion that society doesn't spend money on trying to replicate. Sometimes these chemical instructions (or messages) can feel overwhelmingly negative, but being able to see them as chemical responses and still make a decision to respond to what is going on, rather than how we feel, is a skill that is worth every effort to invest in.

There is very frank and honest science out there about how our brains and bodies interact with the experiences we have when very young, which can affect how these chemical messages flow in later life (Cicchetti and Rogosch, 2012; Campbell, 2010). More recent and very pragmatic neuroscience talks us through how we can work with our brains to actually release different neurochemicals according to our need (Hanson, 2020). This sounds like science fiction but it really isn't (this is just about a simple practice developed thousands of years ago called meditation). There are four main neurochemicals that are worth getting to know and the table below offers a description of each, along with possible example activities from everyday life that help to release that chemical.

Chemical	Feeling	Examples from everyday life
Dopamine	Reward, satisfaction	Completing a task, self-care, eating food, celebrating little wins
Oxytocin	Connection, bonding	Sharing a secret, playing with the dog, giving a compliment
Serotonin	Mood stabiliser	Sunshine, walking in nature, running, swimming, meditating
Endorphin	Pain killer, soother	Laughter, dark chocolate, essential oils, having a good cry

Introducing our chemical messengers (adapted from Table 3 in *The Policing Mind* by Jessica K. Miller, 2022).

10

From Comfort to Growth

Facing Fears Head-On and Leveraging the 'Beginner's Mind'

> 'The farther one gets into the wilderness, the greater is the attraction of its freedom.'
>
> Theodore Roosevelt, US president (1901–9)

Much has been written about it, and the phrase is oft quoted, but what is a 'comfort zone' and why does it matter in the context of being resilient or overcoming adversity?

Every now and then during my life, schoolteachers, coaches, bosses and friends have suggested that I should 'get out of my comfort zone' and, as a result of making this conscious decision, somehow new opportunities will appear and life will be better. Clearly, whether I was in any form of comfort zone then, or now, is a matter of perspective, but given the fact that the definition of comfort suggests many or all of our needs are being met, why would any of us choose to move beyond that safe, familiar space, particularly if the goal or activity that takes us away from where our needs are being met feels distant and unachievable?

It sounds inherently counterintuitive.

Take this book for example. I have never written a book before. I don't need to write a book. This was never part of any great master plan. At all.

So why am I doing it?

Primarily, because friends encouraged me to record some of my experiences, with a view to perhaps helping others think about their own resilience and how they might, armed with a new perspective, better overcome their own challenges.

Easier said than done.

The moment I started writing, I felt completely out of my depth.

Self-doubt about whether there was any need, any point, or if anyone would even read or care about what I wrote, threatened to overwhelm me. It still does, as I realise that this is not just the preserve of writers but is a sentiment so many of us can relate to; something very much linked to the concept of imposter syndrome, which is felt when we venture into territories or spheres that we have yet to even recognise as places where we would find ourselves.

Ergo, life would be a lot simpler, less stressful and without fear or risk if I just stuck to my day job. But, as you will have gathered, I have rarely opted for the easy or obvious path. If what I share helps anyone think differently or better understand or overcome their own trauma, any personal discomfort will have been worth it.

In this case I made a choice; however, not everyone gets a choice. If one is forced from their comfort zone, what happens next, before one reaches the nirvana of positivity and opportunity? Having even a high-level understanding of the concept and process, ideally in advance, helps us prepare for the phases that follow.

Essentially, there are four main zones to the growth concept, each with their own characteristics.

First comes the *comfort zone*. It is here where we feel (clue is in the title) comfortable. Here, we are safe and secure with most or all of our needs being met, and we feel in control, where our brains lapse into a very predictable zone of thinking; thinking which requires little thought and typically involves operating within a few habitual processes. This sounds positive, and for most people it's enough, but this won't get us to self-actualisation or achieving everything we might be able to do in life.

Next comes the *fear zone*. This is primarily where I am in writing the book, where anxiety kicks in and one's self-confidence is challenged. If moving beyond the comfort zone was optional, it's here that many turn back. I've been tempted. Genuinely.

If one can get through the fear, with the level of anxiety and stress not leading to panic, then we can move into the *learning zone*. As mentioned previously, with resilience being fundamentally about our ability to adapt and learn in the face of stress and adversity, this is arguably the most important phase of the cycle, where we reflect on how far we've come already and acquire new skills and experiences to keep growing and moving forward. I'm getting here, slowly.

Once through the learning zone (which never actually ends), we enter the *growth zone*. The journey to get here is likely to have been painful, but in my experience it is a fantastic place to reach. And the beauty of this zone is that (for me at least) it's primarily mental rather than physical. Accepting that there will be bumps in the road, and no plan is likely to survive contact with external factors, over which we have little or no control, is enlightening in and of itself.

With that mindset of being willing to, or at least consciously, leave my comfort zone, experiences have been significantly richer as a result. Some have been painful, and I would rather they were not required, but I have always learned something positive.

This is why I always try to choose the path less travelled and say yes to any and every opportunity that gives me a chance to learn and grow. While this is as true in my professional business and personal life as it was in my military career, my time in uniform provided many opportunities to get comfortable with being uncomfortable.

Given the Gurkhas' history and pedigree as jungle specialists, it was both a daunting yet exciting prospect to follow in their footsteps. Having never spent any time in such an alien environment, travelling to the jungle for the first time was to be a trip where I would be very much out of my comfort zone and where I could guarantee my character and resilience would be tested to the limit – tropical rainforest is harsh and does not suffer fools.

So much about thriving in the jungle, as in life, is about having the right mindset and learning to adapt. Those who fight the jungle's distinct rhythm always suffered; and the more you fight it, the harder life becomes. By accepting the 'rules of the trees' and learning to live in harmony, or as close to it as possible, then this alien world can be a rewarding and fascinating place. The sights, sounds and smells are like nothing else. In the few sun-drenched, sandy clearings it can be scorching and blinding, but just a few steps away, one enters an entirely new, strange world filled with the cacophony of unfamiliar chatter from animals hiding from view.

Unlike secondary jungle, with its thick and often impenetrable vegetation and brackish water, primary jungle is characterised by very tall trees, fresh water and is generally not inhabited by as many critters that could or would like to bite and poison you. So, apart from an abundance of crocodiles near the main waterways, I felt relatively safe. Even the enormous ants that patrolled day and night were not the biting kind, or so we were told.

However, the two animals that did prove to be utterly maddening were mosquitoes and leeches. I was not prepared for the sheer number of them that plagued us 24/7. The constant whine in our ears as mozzies buzzed around seeking their next meal was debilitating. But, while they were extremely annoying, leeches were far stealthier and usually got you before you even realised that they were there.

When a leech bites you, it secretes an anticoagulant to prevent clotting, causing bleeding to continue until it's engorged and drops off, sated. The bites themselves were generally inconvenient rather than dangerous but, given the hot, humid conditions of jungle life, if you couldn't keep the wound clean, infection would quickly take hold. Having watched a few Vietnam-era films in which soldiers used cigarette lighters to burn them off, we learned quickly that this was, in fact, *not* the most sensible way to deal with them. Instead, a dollop of industrial strength army mozzie repellent usually did the trick. Frustratingly, however, their bites were largely undetectable, so it generally ended up being a bloody affair, requiring liberal application of iodine solution to clean the wound.

After every insertion into the trees, either by helicopter or vehicle, there was always an initial period where I found myself in a futile battle to stay clean. But this was the jungle and the longer you fought the inevitable, the longer it took mentally to accept the environment and move through each zone from comfort through to learning. Smell, in particular, became quickly enhanced and such was the extent of this heightened sensitivity that we were able to ascertain from several hundred yards away if someone had freshly laundered clothes or had used toothpaste.

The daily torrential afternoon rain always sapped morale as it penetrated every fibre. So, the importance of keeping at least one set of clothes dry for sleeping in was something we took very seriously indeed. Should they somehow become wet, it could be extremely draining, both mentally and physically, even for the most robust of soldiers. Although I got used to most of the daily jungle tasks, the dawn and dusk routine of changing between day and night clothes was something I never fully embraced. The overpowering stench of ammonia that accompanied putting on one's wet clothes each morning was nauseating. No matter how many times I did it, I still found myself wincing as I gingerly stuck my arms and legs into the cold, damp, rancid cloth.

While the constant and unrelenting buzz of the jungle continues during the day, everything changes at night. Twilight, in particular, was always an incredibly busy and noisy period as diurnal and nocturnal communities handed over responsibilities. At dusk, once the mole crickets, or 'stand to beetles' as they were known to us, had begun their deafening and distinctive buzzing/grinding mating calls, it signalled that we had only 15 minutes or so before inky-black darkness would envelop us, precipitating a final, frantic period of securing our gear or risk losing it until morning, about 12 hours later.

With no ambient light of any kind, it was the darkest environment I have ever encountered, one where I could not even see my hand in front of my face. For some, even this was hugely uncomfortable and more than a little scary. In terms of mindset, rather than seeing this as a threatening situation, I viewed this much more positively; as a chance for the brain to rest and recalibrate, thereby turning a threat into a safety cue for mental nourishment.

For much of the time, we were able to use hammocks, but occasionally, during specific tactical scenarios, we had to sleep on the ground. And while none of us were particularly comfortable lying on the floor, even in primary jungle, shivering in our wet clothes (the tactical situation did not allow a change into dry clothes) as we snatched a few hours' fitful sleep, none of us expected to encounter anything that would do us serious harm. That said, I did experience something during one deployment that still gives me goosebumps: waking up to find something heavy lying on my stomach.

In the pitch-black night, I could see absolutely nothing. All I knew was that something, weighing several kilograms, was on top of me. I could feel its warmth – helpfully, removing snake from the list of potential culprits – and it had a strong musky odour (not mine, before you ask . . .), neither of which helped me work out what it was or what I should do.

I was most definitely straight back in the fear zone.

As I sought to leverage every sense to identify what it could be and which way it was facing, I was becoming more than a little anxious. I tried to keep calm but all I could hear was my heart beating deafeningly in my head, which I was convinced the animal might also be able to hear, and to which it might react negatively. My mind was racing with hundreds of potentially unpleasant outcomes, none of which helped me relax, given that we were several hours from the nearest hospital. All I could do was try to breathe as lightly as possible and hope that it would just go away.

After what seemed like an hour but was probably only five or ten minutes, I felt movement. I squeezed my eyes even tighter shut and held my breath. Turning around on my stomach several times, the weight lifted.

What caused it to get off I'm not sure, but over the noise of my heart, I heard the animal (whatever it was) break through the foliage and disappear. Welcome to the jungle!

Choosing one's battles and being comfortable with not knowing all the answers, both of which are markers of resilience, have proven to be useful life skills, well beyond the jungle. If we can make the conscious choice of where to deploy our resources, this can supercharge our resilience. It's another way of accepting we don't know or don't necessarily need to know or understand everything to be able to accept a situation and work with it. The beginner's mind is something we can all leverage.

One of my least enjoyable jungle experiences over the years involved an activity called a swamp march – an activity to test even the most tolerant of people. And, yes, a jungle swamp is as hideous a place to be as it sounds. Jungle movement could be difficult at the best of times, but navigating mangrove swamps while carrying full equipment could reduce progress to only a few hundred yards per day. This presented a mental challenge all on its own, as the effort required far outweighed the progress one was able to make.

The water among the gnarled roots was invariably brackish and the mud in which the trees grew was foetid and sticky. Although the reason for ever setting foot in this hellhole was to avoid detection, colourful language occasionally drifted across the stiflingly hot, stale air, indicating growing frustrations as each of us took turns to lose our footing.

On this occasion, as darkness fell, we reached our intended destination (which looked the same as every other part of the swamp, to be honest) and hurried to find a suitable harbour location that we could defend; not that anybody would have been likely to follow us in, given how unpleasant it was. No sooner had we settled down for the night, a strange buzzing noise filled the air, quietly at first, but growing louder by the minute. This was not the familiar 'stand to beetle'. Eventually, whatever it was appeared to be above us, now vibrating at an ear-splittingly high decibel level. If this had been a sci-fi movie, I would not have been surprised if we'd then been illuminated by bright lights before being abducted and whisked away in an alien spaceship. Instead, we found ourselves beneath a giant swarm of hornets. Had any of us been stung by even a handful of these beasts, it would have been very serious. Luckily, after maybe 15 minutes, the swarm began to move off and we breathed a sigh of relief, not that it gave many of us much cause to relax.

Cut off entirely from civilisation and often going for days without being able to see further than a few feet, it was an experience that placed most of us well outside our comfort zones. But with the fast-paced nature of life today, I look back with fondness on those periods spent largely disconnected. Although mentally and physically exhausting, it was a simpler, slower time.

As a jungle warfare instructor, I was often required to train others, putting soldiers through their paces in a safe learning environment, thereby enabling them to move into their own respective growth zones.

Unlike relatively clean primary jungle, secondary jungle is a far less straightforward affair. You really have to keep your wits about you. At one end of the scale there were panthers, crocodiles and jaguar, through to highly venomous snakes, scorpions and spiders at the other. I was keen to meet none of them, ever. One of the most venomous snakes to live in that part of the world is a pit viper called a Fer-de-Lance. Locally, it's known as the '20-minute snake' because, according to them, if a victim is unable to receive an antidote within 20 minutes, they are very likely to die. Given that much of our work was taking place at least 45 minutes' helicopter flight from the nearest base, this gave us little comfort, even if local estimates about the snake's lethality were exaggerated.

Not only is the Fer-de-Lance highly venomous, it's also territorial and aggressive. Perfect. Thankfully, I only ever encountered one in the wild, but it was quite the experience. As I navigated our Land Rover along a sandy track on the jungle fringe, I stumbled across an adult snake sunning itself in the middle of the road. But rather than retreating as most snakes would, I was shocked to see it turn and move rapidly towards me, before striking out several times at my now stationary vehicle before retreating. I wouldn't have been surprised if it had pulled out a flick knife and demanded that I hand over my wallet.

Away from the jungle, military parachuting provided many examples of being forced well outside of my comfort zone. Whether conducting freefall training with oxygen and equipment at night, parachuting from just a few thousand feet into the sea, or from only a few hundred feet underneath the British Army's low-level parachute – where the time to deal with malfunctions before you hit the ground is minimal – the importance of taking the training seriously was critical.

I am not sure that knowing any of this as a child would necessarily have helped me deal with the very early trauma, but everything that followed now makes much more sense to me in the context of this model. Learning is never over; every day we wake up and have the capacity to grow. But the path is not necessarily linear.

Every time I sense that I am entering the fear zone, I know that it's just a natural phase through which I need to pass to reach the learning and growth zones. This alone helps me let go of those things over which I have no control and focus instead on those I can shape and influence, the most important of which is a positive, growth mindset.

PRACTICAL TECHNIQUE: 'FEAR VS THREAT'

In this chapter we have explored what it feels like to be faced with the fearful prospect of the unknown. Sometimes, it's natural to feel fear, but it may not always be necessary. Sometimes, we just need to tap into our own innate capacity to handle that which we find proportionately threatening. A good way of differentiating between fear and threat is to use the FEAR and THREAT mnemonics, introduced in Chapter 3: FEAR (**F**alse **E**vidence **A**ppearing **R**eal) and THREAT (**T**rustworthy, **H**eightened **R**esponse, **E**ffective and **T**actical). Experiencing fear is an uncomfortable sensation, and managing threat is direct action. It's helpful to remind ourselves that we can follow the former with the latter.

Science and Thinking

Comfort zone

A sense of comfort can come from that to which we default and that to which we become familiar. Unfortunately, just because we default to something or find it familiar is not to say in any way that it is necessarily good for us at any one time; sometimes it is very important to step out of our comfort zone to adapt to our environment. We have spoken before about our 'Default Mode Network' in the brain. When we need to move on in life, as we develop from childhood (Tian et al., 2022) or adapt to new situations or ways of living in adulthood, it's important to know that what we have conditioned ourselves to think can be sticky and it takes effort to break new ground (Keysers and

Gazzola, 2014), but it is possible. What is more, the good news from neuroscience is not just that we can rewire our thinking to help us move from comfort to growth, but also that there are many ways in which the brain really likes this. The concept of 'novelty and reward' has long been studied (Costa et al., 2014) and we know now that noting the newness of something we have brought about can release those feel-good chemicals (such as dopamine), which will reward us for the effort we made and encourage us to do it more when it works out well. In practical terms, moving from comfort to growth requires some mental effort, determination and courage. We can prime the brain to be receptive to the later reward by simply saying to oneself, 'I've got this'. Psychologist duo Forrest and Rick Hanson put this another way: 'Booking your win.' (a suggestion that regularly features in their podcast, Being Well*). We can take it further by consciously acknowledging that we have what we need to make this step, be it physical protection or strength, the team you are with or the required knowledge and skills. In this way, we create our own comfort as we move towards growth – and doing so is already mental growth in itself!*

11

Carrying the Weight of Loss: Making Sense of Trauma

Gaining Perspective and Taking Time to Reflect

'Grief is the price we pay for love.'

Her Majesty Queen Elizabeth II

Loss and its aftermath can be a particularly traumatic time in one's life, but what constitutes loss is deeply personal and how one copes with it varies markedly from individual to individual. We all experience grief and trauma differently and recognising this is vital for self-compassion.

For some, loss may relate to a bereavement, for others it could be a job, a relationship, independence, mobility, a medical condition, cherished possession or perhaps an identity. Whatever the realm in which we experience loss, we can practise accepting, dealing with and managing that felt sense of loss, and build constructive thought processes to apply to other manifestations of loss we may encounter.

I don't pretend to have experienced every one of these, but having spent time supporting those who do, I can certainly empathise.

In my case, sustaining several permanent disabilities from my military service, losing more than 60 friends and colleagues killed in action, being denied once in a lifetime experiences with my daughter too numerous to count, as well as experiencing the pain of miscarriage and the deaths of close friends and family, are all losses that have affected me, each playing a part in sharpening the lens through which I now view the world.

Every loss, funeral or memorial has left a mark, not least for the innocent families and friends left behind to grieve.

While nothing will ever completely fill the void following such events, I've attempted to approach life with an overwhelming sense of gratitude, hope and perspective, aware that there are always others facing more difficult challenges than mine. Each day, therefore, is an opportunity to make a positive difference; focusing on those things I can influence and worrying less about those I cannot. This, like so much in life, remains a work in progress because it's hard.

I am also deeply aware that for some, who've not found themselves routinely out of their comfort zone or facing adversity, their ability to handle loss or adversity may be less well developed. As such, dealing with the associated trauma is likely to be more challenging or even overwhelming, if facing it without the protective shield that years of resilience building brings.

Although I've been lucky (or unlucky) enough to have plenty of opportunities to develop my own protective shield, there have been many occasions where I've been tested; times when I have found it challenging to maintain a positive mindset and focus on navigating a way through. Nobody is impervious.

Perhaps surprisingly, more visceral for me than any physical losses

I've encountered has been the loss of time. Time stolen that can never be recovered.

The personal realisation that time with one's children could be restricted or denied came as a huge shock. It's a story one reads about only in the news. It's something that happens to other people. It's not something that happens to you.

Until it does.

And when it happened to me, my whole world collapsed.

Even now, after nearly 17 years of being able to measure time together with my daughter only in days and weeks, I become emotional. All I had ever wanted was to be a dad; a really good dad, willing and able to provide a safe, loving, secure environment within which my children could grow, flourish and achieve their full potential. Sadly, the script in my mind's eye was written for someone else.

However, despite crippling financial and emotional challenges, compounded by over ten thousand miles separating us, we have much to be grateful for. Even though our time together is still painfully short, we have always made every second count, and while we organise exciting experiences, we also love just *being*. Routine things that most parents give little thought to – grocery shopping, bath-time, hugs, bedtime stories or the school run – are the inconsequential events that are genuinely anticipated for months in advance and cherished for weeks afterwards.

So, while those who know the full story may feel that I have legitimate reasons to be angry and frustrated, that wouldn't really help, not least because this is all my daughter has ever known; our unusual circumstance is actually her 'normal'. Instead, therefore, we focus on the positives of making memories and looking to a brighter future; a future filled with new adventures and greater freedoms.

Having come so far, I know that we are both at a point where we can and will keep moving forward, accepting that a few more scars along the way are likely, if not inevitable, but each one will be worth it as they'll point to a lesson learned or challenge overcome. However, the shock of hearing a sobbing child ask if they might be in trouble for loving both parents, or asking for experiences rather than physical gifts would be devastating for any parent. Nothing prepared me for that.

Something else that has surprised me, about which I have only become conscious since becoming a parent, but I recognise might well be due to other factors, is that my emotions live far closer to the surface than they ever used to. Upsetting situations, particularly those involving children, whether in real life or in film, trigger emotional reactions that would have been entirely alien to me before the birth of my daughter.

While becoming a parent did not mean I changed how I approached operational missions or the balance of risk, I did become more aware of the impact of conflict on children. And when innocent children are caught in the middle of conflicts not of their own making, it can be extremely damaging and upsetting, ill-equipped as their young brains are to process what is going on around them.

On another occasion, I deployed on a night helicopter operation with a coalition unit. While there was nothing to suggest that this was going to be more dangerous than any other missions in the previous weeks, as we approached our designated HLS the sky lit up with bright flashes and explosions. We couldn't see it from the back of our helicopter, but a group of armed men had run from the target building, several of whom had opened fire.

The response from the helicopter gunships had been swift, firing salvos of rockets to neutralise the immediate threat, thereby providing enough of a window for us to land safely. Once deposited, the helicopters lifted quickly and disappeared back into the starry sky, leaving us with the sound of stray dogs barking angrily in the distance. Given the relatively isolated nature of this particular target, half the team would secure and search the building – likely housing the women and children – with another team tasked to locate the men seen running into the fields beyond.

Leveraging thermal imaging technology, one of the teams found two of the men who'd shot at the aircraft hiding in vegetation by a deep drainage ditch and, after an exchange of fire, both were killed. Concurrently, the airborne surveillance aircraft scoured the area, looking for the third male.

With my heart racing, our team was directed towards a faint heat source in the middle of the field next to the target house. We needed to check if this was someone lying very still, partially covered to avoid detection, or perhaps a cow or other animal asleep among the crops.

As we crept forward through the tall grass towards the potentially armed insurgent, the body of an adult male came into focus. Given recent experience, where insurgents had pretended to be dead only to detonate suicide vests or throw grenades when coalition troops got close, we moved with extreme caution.

After observing at a safe distance for a few minutes, none of us could identify any movement, so we went forward to inspect. The airborne surveillance operator's instinct had been right: this was indeed the body of a man, lying flat on his back. It appeared that he'd taken a direct hit from one of the helicopters, resulting in a catastrophic brain injury.

In the grass next to his outstretched hands lay a blue Nokia mobile phone alongside a packet of Marlboro cigarettes with its distinctive red-and-white packaging. Having positively identified him as the target of the operation, we headed back to the house to link up with the rest of the team.

Inside, I joined those chatting with a group of women and children.

Despite the unwelcome wake-up call, resulting in the frantic exits of their fathers and uncles, the kids were all very chirpy and friendly, laughing and joking.

Although confident that we'd accounted for the insurgent leader, now lying just a few hundred feet away, we wanted to gain additional confirmation, if possible, from the families. As was often the case, the women were reluctant to talk, but the children were far more open and keen to practise their English. One of the boys, who couldn't have been more than ten years old, approached me and started reeling off the lines he'd learned from American movies.

After spending a few minutes chatting, I asked if his dad had been at the house and if he might have been one of the men who had run off. He said, yes, his dad had run out before we arrived. To ascertain which, if any, of the men outside might be his father, I asked if his dad had a phone or if he smoked. He confirmed, enthusiastically, that his dad did indeed smoke 'red- and white-ones' and that he had a 'blue phone'.

My heart sank.

I still find it difficult to think about it today, even though there was nothing realistically that we could have done differently, and it was his own father who'd put himself and his children in that situation. But the fact that this innocent boy's life would change forever the moment we left, once they'd found the body, upset me. This would be a physical and emotional loss for him that would never heal. What support could he expect? Very little, if any. I still wonder what became of that poor child and many like him; all innocent victims having to deal with loss or trauma far too young.

As was the case on this occasion and many others like it (I know this may sound silly), whenever I experienced something disturbing, I consciously reminded myself that such scenes were not normal. Normalising the abhorrent is not a way to authentically maintain cognitive resilience. We may acclimate to repeated exposure to acute stress as part of our occupation or personal life conditions, but this is not the same as telling our brain that what we experience is normal. To maintain our integrity and our faith in being human, we have to deliberately remind ourselves that each time we see something abhorrent, that it is so.

I remembered to be shocked, as I was hyper-vigilant that if I ever stopped feeling any emotion after witnessing trauma, I probably needed to speak to someone or seek professional help. I'd read too many accounts of soldiers, firefighters, law enforcement and health professionals for whom continued exposure had numbed them to the point that they no longer felt anything.

As a leader, I knew that I needed to remain in touch with my own senses and emotions so that I could better support those for whom I was responsible or who might be struggling. The fact that I was shaken and saddened after speaking to that young boy I took as a good sign – at least I hadn't checked out.

Every event has the power to wound, but because of the nature of trauma and loss, those carrying the greatest weight are often far away and completely disconnected from the incident that caused it.

Following a particularly tragic mission, resulting in the loss of 19 servicemen along with their aircraft, the unit to which I was attached effectively ran out of people to carry coffins for the repatriation ceremony. As a liaison officer and former pilot, I was asked if I'd be willing to carry the body of one of the aircrew. It was an honour I could not refuse.

As we stood to attention and the aircraft ramp was raised, I could feel the warmth of tears on my cheeks in the dusty evening air. I hadn't known any of the deceased personally but that didn't matter. We were, and remain, part of a brother- and sisterhood that transcends nationality, ethnicity and everything else, and I could think only of the families – sons, daughters, mothers, fathers, brothers, sisters and countless additional friends and family, for whom the arrival of this flight would mark the start of a long and very painful journey.

The sight of 19 coffins in neat rows in the back of the aircraft, wrapped in their national flag, was a heartbreaking image, seared in my memory, frozen in time.

During another army deployment I was privileged to find myself working with some of the bravest yet most traumatised soldiers I'd ever encountered, who were having a particularly torrid time fighting in a violent, baking hot hellhole of a place.

Such had been the tempo and ferocity of the fight in their area of operations (AO) that statisticians had worked out that in some bases every time a soldier left the safety of their compound to go on a patrol, there was a one in four chance they could be killed or lose a limb to an IED. With these appalling odds, quite understandably, many soldiers were sick with fear – some literally – knowing that the very next mission might be their last. This presented a considerable leadership and moral challenge for commanders, as they sought to inspire their soldiers to follow them, by reminding them constantly of the higher common purpose: the 'Why?'.

Having endured so much loss, with little time to deal with the psychological impact of witnessing their friends and colleagues killed or sustaining life-changing physical injuries, being a guest in this battlegroup's extremely austere home was a strange place to be. On the one hand, the soldiers were incredibly upbeat, but there was also a palpable sense of lingering grief in the air: soldiers with tortured faces and thousand-yard stares, reliving over and over the trauma of recent attacks, mental and physical wounds yet to heal.

With each sunset gathering on the helipad, where those killed in action were given a military send off, the bonds between the soldiers who remained grew stronger.

The sounding of the Last Post has always been very moving, never failing to send goosebumps down my spine, but since then, it holds even deeper meaning for me. Each time I hear it, years later, I am immediately transported back to the sights, sounds and emotions of that deployment and the other places from where we were unable to bring everyone home.

With each passing incident, young men and women were forced to grow up far too quickly, innocence stolen, pain and grief etched visibly a little deeper. Too many accommodation blocks, where soldiers once were crammed together in close-knit teams, now sported empty bed spaces. Green camp cots, still with dust and sweat stains, were reminders of where friends and comrades once lay; those who'd either made the ultimate sacrifice or who'd been flown home for life-saving medical treatment, unlikely to return.

It was important, therefore, for my team to find ways to support the commander and his leadership team in their quest to maintain the troop's fighting spirit and morale, and take the battle to the enemy.

Despite the difficulty of working in such a high-pressure environment I saw countless examples of inspirational leadership. One senior officer chose repeatedly to join his men and women on patrol, even though his role within the battlegroup didn't require him to do so. We spoke at length about why he was doing it and he answered simply: he wanted to show the soldiers, regardless of role, rank or gender, that he was no better than them and that he was willing to lead from the front. Selfless, visible acts such as this were incredibly powerful ways to give confidence to those who might be struggling mentally or emotionally.

Tragically, he was killed in action, in typically selfless style, carrying the stretcher of another critically injured soldier to the emergency medical evacuation helicopter, leaving behind a wife and two young girls, with whom I am now friends. If he could see how they have flourished, and how he continues to inspire and influence their lives, I have no doubt he'd be bursting with pride. Sadly, he was one of many hundreds seriously wounded or killed during that deployment.

Spending time with the unit commander, I saw at first hand the toll every loss of a soldier took on him and his people. He carried the weight of all his losses bravely, but personally and painfully, obviously.

Each time we heard the 'crump' of a distant explosion from within the relative safety of the blast-proof operations centre we held our breaths, fearing the worst but hoping for the best. On several occasions when this played out, I caught the commander's eye and could clearly see the fear in his eyes, living as we all were in a constant state of apprehension.

The commander's empathy and love for his people was evident for all to see, but every new death or serious injury affected him deeply. An inspiration and rock for so many, he shouldered a disproportionate share of the burden. Such is the lot of a leader.

Being one of the last stops in the operational area, resupply convoys had to be planned carefully to avoid enemy ambushes, travelling therefore at some risk. Knowing soldiers were putting their lives in danger to bring fresh water and food made all of us think very carefully about waste. Drinking only half a water bottle and throwing the rest away, for example, was considered a crime, as signs reminded everyone that once the water ran out, others would be putting their lives on the line to replenish it. When convoys made it through without incident, not only was there obvious relief, but also palpable excitement as to what treats might have made it through with the essentials.

It's funny what you crave when denied creature comforts. For me, particularly in hot operational theatres, it was always cold milk. After a convoy resupply, we were blessed with one or two days of 'real' UHT milk, before switching back to a lesser powdered substitute, until the next convoy arrived. Although powdered milk made with lukewarm water may not sound appealing, it's amazing how quickly we all learned to adapt, accept the conditions and find ways to see positives in the most basic of luxuries.

I was also reminded, day in, day out, of the importance of maintaining perspective and an appreciation for the bigger picture. What struck me working with some of the most dedicated soldiers I would encounter in my career was that no matter how difficult things became, none of them ever gave up. They kept fighting for the mission, for each other and for those friends they'd lost, to whom they owed so much.

How each of us experiences, deals with and (hopefully) moves on from trauma is a very personal matter. Some are better at it than others, but all of us can learn tools and techniques that can help us. For those facing the most extreme forms of trauma or loss, more work may be required to build confidence and resilience, but it's all possible.

I am lucky to have recognised those activities that bring me joy and hope, even in the darkest of situations.

Getting out of the house and into nature is often all that's required. A short walk by a river or among trees can do wonders. Alternatively, taking a few minutes to watch a beautiful sunrise or sunset, exercising and getting sweaty, raising funds for causes I care deeply about and supporting charities who provide life-changing services to those most in need, listening to music, or just sitting still for a moment (rare!) to paint or draw brings me immense joy, offsetting the horrors encountered along the way. The other lifesaver during those darkest moments came from my most loyal supporter – Maia – my amazing German Shorthaired Pointer. At the time of writing, recently passed away, shortly after reaching (rather amazingly) her seventeenth birthday. Without her by my side during some of the most challenging periods, having travelled with me to live in Australia, North America and beyond, I don't know where I'd be today. Genuinely.

The final story I'll share concerning this period relates to another operation to detain an insurgent leader in a place far from home.

Driving from our base, we left a small team with our vehicles in a defensive position, before travelling the rest of the distance on foot. The ground made for fast movement, allowing us to reach the small cluster of farm buildings more quickly than we'd anticipated. After finding weapons and other evidence that corroborated the intelligence we had been provided by our army analysts, the target was arrested.

Everything had gone exceptionally smoothly and, achieving success without use of force, we began the patrol back to our vehicles. Although we did not anticipate a particularly high IED threat in this area, the terrain meant it was safer to move in single-file formation.

Our vehicles now in sight, I could see patrol members taking up defensive positions around their vehicles, where they would stay until the last man arrived safely.

I too would soon be back in my own vehicle and we would be on our way home.

As I began to think about the journey ahead, I was blinded by a bright light and hit simultaneously with the heat, shockwave and ear-splitting noise of an explosion directly in front of me.

An involuntary reaction saw me drop immediately onto my haunches and turn my head away from the seat of the blast. As my face and arms were peppered by thousands of small stones, I felt like a pin cushion. Simultaneously, I was enveloped in an unexpected misty wetness that my brain could not quite process.

Once the dust began to settle, I looked up.

Through my NVGs, I could see grainy green flashes of movement as some of the team ran between the vehicles. I sensed that people were shouting but I could hear none of it as my head was filled with a high-pitched tone that drowned out all other sounds.

A rapid visual scan of the ground in front of me confirmed the worst.

Where one of our local partner force officers had been walking a few feet ahead of me just a split-second before, there was now a large crater. I could not quite make out what remained of him, but I doubted he could have survived such a blast; my focus had to switch to thinking about protecting the rest of the team.

Fearing that we had inadvertently strayed into a minefield, I screamed as loudly as I could for everyone to stop moving and stay exactly where they were. Although I couldn't tell if I was making any sound, given the whining still filling every part of my head, it seemed to work, and all movement ceased. Later, my colleagues explained that they had not seen the blast and had assumed instead that we were under attack from enemy mortars, hence seeking to get to the safety of our armoured vehicles.

Having been around or involved in several other explosive incidents, this seemed a lot larger than a standard anti-personnel mine, so the assumption had to be that there were anti-tank mines in the area, which could be, as evidenced, far more devastating.

Still struggling to hear anything, I put out a radio message directing that nobody was to move until the mine-clearance team had confirmed that the area around them was safe. One IED detector was already up with the vehicles ahead and another was behind me somewhere towards the rear of the patrol.

Still in a crouch, performing what was probably the longest squat I have ever managed, I tried not to move, for fear that even the most minute transference of weight would be all that was required to trigger a pressure plate attached to another bomb.

As my eyes grew more accustomed to the dark, I could now clearly see my colleague, Jim, who'd been patrolling immediately in front of me. He was lying on the ground, groaning, trying to speak. The fact that he was conscious and calling my name, begging me to help him, was a good sign. We were always taught to take more interest in and prioritise those who were unconscious or not making any sense. In this case, he was talking lucidly, albeit with some difficulty.

As I passed the light of a small torch over his body, I could see that all his limbs were still attached and there were no obvious open wounds or catastrophic haemorrhage, which was a relief. But his face gave me cause for concern. It was covered in blood and, although I couldn't make out the source of the bleeding, it was clear he needed treatment. Jim said he couldn't see, which was obviously extremely worrying for him, but it was not yet obvious if his vision was being obscured temporarily by grit or blood, or whether he might have been blinded; a very real possibility given how close he was to the detonation.

I desperately wanted to move and provide potentially life-saving treatment, but I had to wait for what felt like an eternity as the mine-clearing team made their way methodically from the rear of the patrol to check for IEDs, first around me, then Jim.

In the meantime, I continued to keep him calm by telling him that I could not see any major blood loss, that he would be OK and that we just had to wait a few more minutes until I could reach him safely.

Having radioed back to our base operations room that we had been involved in an IED incident, they were standing by to send whatever medical or other fire support we needed. Once the IED detector operator had cleared and marked a safe path to us and several feet around us, we were able to step forward to give Jim the medical attention he needed.

Moving next to the blast crater, it was now obvious that our local partner had been killed instantly and would not have felt a thing, although this provided little comfort. We had lost one of our men and that was devastating.

Just a few feet away from the crater, I found his head and shoulders.

Although the blast had been powerful enough to ensure much of his body had simply vanished, everything that remained appeared untouched. Looking at his face, one might have assumed he was sleeping. His helmet was still in place, eyes closed with not a single obvious cut or scratch on him.

As I tried to picture the scene when his family would be informed of their loss, I could think only of the importance in Islamic culture of being able to bury their loved ones within 24 hours. I became laser-focused on trying to find as much of his body as I could, so that we would be able to hand over something for them to bury and mourn.

While the team doctor continued to work to stabilise Jim, which would determine the type of medical extraction we requested, I grabbed a large plastic bag. After taking care to place Mohammed's head and shoulders inside, I began to search the area away from the mine crater to ensure we didn't inadvertently leave anything behind.

As I was beginning to lose hope that I would be able to recover anything else, I found a lower limb around 200 feet from the main blast area. While the leg that had triggered the device was almost certainly destroyed, his trailing leg was severed cleanly below the knee. The area of the traumatic amputation had been cauterised in the blast and, although the trousers were gone, his foot was still secure inside a fully laced boot, seemingly with no damage whatsoever.

Despite the disturbing nature of my combat experiences, I have been extremely fortunate not to have suffered any obvious debilitating ill effects from my service. But that night, having to place my colleague's remains, still warm, into a plastic bag is something that did affect me. Not because of what I was doing, but I was wracked with worry that seeing him like this would be too much for his family to bear.

However, as any combat commander knows, when you are responsible for the safety and well-being of your team, that becomes your absolute focus.

This incident was no different.

I was in the zone and had to suppress my natural human emotions until much later. Nothing was going to bring him back, but I felt hopeful that, by taking the time and making every effort to honour him, Mohammed's family would be grateful for the opportunity to perform a proper burial.

Meanwhile, our doctor informed me that, while Jim's injuries were serious, he was stable and could be extracted. Although we were still very much in enemy territory and at risk, I found myself trying to fight off the wave of exhaustion that comes when severely heightened levels of adrenaline drop back down to normal. It was a relief to arrive home without further incident and I handed over the remains to his unit commander, who would make the final journey with him to be reunited with his family.

When I think of this incident, I am reminded about the privilege and pressure of leadership and how personally I took the responsibility. While this incident is at the extreme end of what most people experience in their daily lives, trauma takes many forms and the ways in which the brain responds, or can be trained to respond, yields valuable lessons for the everyday. I've certainly used what I learned from battle in much more ordinary, if no less traumatic, situations. I am also now more aware that being able to move beyond trauma and grow is a process; a necessary process the brain must go through and, therefore, taking time to understand what is happening inside our own brains can be extremely helpful.

With hindsight, I can now identify the ways in which I tried to process such a traumatic event and make sense of the experience: gaining perspective; using smart compassion; checking in with my decision-making; and seeing the bigger picture by not only remembering what is important to me but also what is important to others. I did my best to reflect on my own thought processes in an objective way, rather than getting caught up in them. But what was going on in my brain?

I gathered details to create a big pot of memory around the incident, in a similar way to the taking of statements in a police investigation, or the recording of details for insurance purposes after a road accident.

Creating an overhead view is also used in some types of trauma therapy, to help generate context and perspective for those who literally need some space from the incident that is troubling them. I've since learned that this is what my brain is doing when I describe what would look like a 'snake' of people when viewing them from above, although that wasn't a deliberate turn of phrase on my part. By including some of the more neutral information about the environment and the significance of a place, e.g. returning the body of my colleague to his family and his village, the brain is recognising what's important to others. I'm focusing on my sensory experience and tuning into my emotional response to stay in the moment. By seeing each experience afresh and trying not to become numb or blind to it helps maintain values and integrity and, ultimately, resilience. Exercising gratitude and compassion helps regulate fear and can work to reduce one's own stress response.

Establishing perspective is one of the most important things that our minds can do, as it helps us to make sense of traumatic incidents and move on from them, thereby maintaining our resilience. However, when something really threatening happens, the amygdala in our brain releases lots of stress toxins to galvanise the body into action, so we are able to meet the demands of the situation. Over time, these toxins can erode the hippocampus (it only has a thin layer of cells around it), which can stop it from working effectively. This can be extremely frustrating, as when we really need to get some perspective, the very part of the brain that we rely on to help with this is being affected by our own stress. This is why those who are continually exposed to trauma can become worse at processing it, leading to debilitating conditions such as PTSD.

Thankfully, it doesn't have to be this way. Not for everyone.

Regular exposure to acute stress and threat to life as part of our vocation may be something we have to learn to accept, but the abhorrent acts engaged in by others are not something we should normalise. We need to maintain our values to sustain our resilience, otherwise we feel lost and numb. We also need to acknowledge the meaningfulness in what we do, and sometimes that means accepting the fact that we must face that which we find abhorrent in the line of duty or in our daily lives. Calling out to our brain when something is wrong is a meaningful process and it protects us. We can learn to activate the hippocampus and apply the perspective of space and time to incidents that we find hard. This way, we can let that area of the brain do its stuff, put the experience into context, file the memory and turn off that alarm. We do this by activating the spatial ('where') and the episodic ('when') to make sense of events and move on.

The biggest take away for me on that night, as on so many other similar occasions, was the importance of making sensible and balanced judgements, often very quickly and under pressure. In this instance, hearing and watching Jim ask me to help him, just a few feet in front of me, and not doing so, was tough. Had I moved to help him and stepped on another IED or anti-tank mine, I would almost certainly have killed us both and others nearby. That would have been unforgivable.

That said – and I have given this considerable thought over the years, particularly as I have become more involved in mental health charity work and campaigns – if my failure to provide urgent care had led to Jim's death, only for us later to discover (as we did) that there were no additional IEDs, that would be something I believe I would struggle to deal with; having not acted to save a life.

PRACTICAL TECHNIQUE: 'THERE IS'

In this chapter we have explored what it is like to experience an overwhelming sense of loss, grief and trauma. There are many ways in which we can learn over time to process the enormity of how we feel in such circumstances . . . but perhaps the most immediate thing we can do is get a little objectivity. One way of doing this without trivialising or negating what we feel is to simply put our feelings into a bigger melting pot; a more objective, aggregated context. Rather than thinking, 'I feel sad' or 'I can't do this', translate these thoughts into different phrases which are equally true: '*There is* sadness' and '*There is* overwhelm/self-doubt'. This is a very subtle distinction but one you can really feel in your brain and body when you practice it. There are these feelings in the world and sometimes we taste them.

Science and Thinking

Grief and loss

As mentioned before, grief that is complicated by trauma exposure can lead to a state of living in what seems like a 'provisional existence' (Frankl, 1946), yet, overall, grief is widely explained as being a process rather than a particular state. The best-known work on this is by Kübler-Ross (On Death and Dying, 1969), whose guidance is compassionate, but very pragmatic, and on which much exploration on loss is built. We all experience grief and traumatic grief differently as individuals. The understanding that brains have different experiences is recognised in the scientific realm (O'Connor and Arizmendi, 2014), but it's also important for us as everyday folk living our lives to understand that grief and loss can show up in different ways, too. At any one time, any of us might be grieving or sensing a loss of our identity or status, of our plans for the future, of connections we have with others or of our physical health. Thankfully, the same constructive thought processes that we might use with grief can be applied to any sense of loss.

There are practical meditations available to help with a whole manner of life experiences, helping us relax our attachment to material things, certain identities or status, and ideas that aren't always helpful for us (Burke et al., 2010). In Buddhist psychology, the concept of loss is inextricably linked to our understanding of transience and impermanence, or in other words 'things change'. When we are used to that idea of repeatedly riding the waves of adversity and relief, we grow an innate sense that, whether we like it or not, nothing lasts forever. It is no wonder perhaps that the old adage 'This too will pass' offers such relief to so many. This is not to deny that change can be painful or to trivialise it. I find it helpful to add to this thought the caveat I once heard: 'This too shall pass . . . it might pass like a kidney stone, but it will pass.' If we feel things too personally sometimes, we can widen our perspective and apply this sense of impermanence to the social world around us; times change culturally too, they simply do (Gesimer et al., 2022).

Finding meaning after trauma

Abhorrent acts engaged in by others are not things we should normalise. To do so, especially in a work or occupation situation, would be to put ourselves at risk of what has come to be known as 'moral injury' (Greenberg et al., 2020), wherein we can suffer by means of association with the decision-making or behaviours of others with which we do not agree or personally find immoral. As we mentioned before, when this happens, the stakes for our self-worth are high. It has long been understood that having values feels good, it makes us feel as if we have something stronger than us to hold us up, hence the adage, 'They who stand for nothing fall for anything'. Recent research in UK policing (Burchell et al., 2023) has shown that meaningfulness in what we do can protect us against the suffering and trauma exposure that could otherwise lead to clinical levels of Complex Post-Traumatic Stress Disorder (the University of Cambridge study also showed that those officers who didn't retain a sense of meaning in their work were twice as likely to develop Complex PTSD, a condition which affects at least 12 per cent of serving UK police, and PTSD another 8 per cent). Calling out to our brain what is meaningful to us helps to maintain resilience in the most adverse of situations. Having values is not for the faint-hearted, but they enable us to gain the mental strength and stamina needed to take on what life may throw at us. So, how can we use our thinking skilfully to achieve this?

One practical approach is to be open to the moments where we find value, and then to absorb them into us as a resource. It is perhaps worth noting that this absorption is very different from weaponising our values, by becoming militant in our actions because we follow a certain rhetoric. This is about having a felt sense of being aligned with what makes us feel good and decent and worthwhile, and is less about the behaviour or actions of others. We have mentioned the HEAL technique (Hanson, 2013) before and this is a great one to use here. If we can learn to almost pounce on a moment whereby we have a glimmer of satisfaction, or the sense of things around us or things spoken hitting the spot and reminding us who we are, we can then link this to what we believe is meaningful. It could be as simple as **H***aving an exchange with a random stranger about a topic that means something to us;* **E***nriching it by noticing how it feels in the body to be aligned with someone who gets us and what we value;* **A***bsorbing it by really indulging in the moment and committing it to memory and to your sense of who you are deep inside, as a bright reminder that you know who you are and what you believe in. The optional final step is to* **L***ink this feeling of strength and meaning to times or exchanges with people you have shared before, which have either left you feeling a) the opposite (bereft, disarmed and disconnected), thereby neutralising those feelings or b) similar (where you have felt enamoured and empowered and connected), thereby further reinforcing this positive association.*

Dissociation and somatic work

Dissociation and numbness is a common trait reported by those repeatedly exposed to traumatic experiences and one that affects over a third of even healthy police officers in the UK (Brewin et al., 2022). Dissociative disorders are also a major concern in contemporary psychiatry in relation to military service (Boyd et al., 2018). Those working under extreme or traumatic conditions can become used to dissociating, ignoring some sensory feedback and defaulting to concentrating on decision-making in what becomes a very cerebral world. Reconnecting with our bodies and acknowledging the legitimacy of the chemical messages we are receiving (interpreted as emotions) is a progressive area of therapy for trauma, known as 'somatic' (Winblad et al., 2018). As we have mentioned before, work by Bessel Van der Kolk (2014) is a great place to start to understand how early life experiences that may have been difficult can make our experiences of being in a body in adult life more problematic.

A great practical technique for managing dissociation comes from an observation of a police constable who became involved in police trauma resilience work by the charity Police Care UK. The response officer's family had noticed over time that there was a clear distinction in his behaviour each day, based on what he did with his boots. If he left his boots at the door, the officer was usually open and receptive to the family, fully engaging and communicative, tactile with them and generally all present and correct, as it were. However, if his boots remained on his feet as he entered the house, the family soon got to know that his frame of mind was such that he was still in work mode and was not ready yet to engage. The job was still in his head as well as his feet. After a while both the officer and his family recognised that there was something to be said for 'Boots at the door'; they shared the understanding that the boots were the key to where he was associating at the time. If they were on, he was mentally at work. If they were off, with his own feet on the floor, he was grounded, present and all there for them to engage with. For the officer, having his feet firmly on the floor and feeling the carpet below was also a way to come back into his body and begin a process of letting go of the tension he'd been holding, bit by bit, from toes to head. As discussed already, a simple body scan meditation or a sleep relaxation technique can help us achieve the same. But, first, we need to work out what our tell is for when we are dissociating and are somewhere else in our mind.

Military resilience: survival and agility

The fact that surviving an incident when others haven't can be extremely challenging is well understood in everyday life, especially if those others are known to us or are people for whom we cared. The term 'survivors' guilt' is commonly heard and yet there is a certain sparsity of research into survivors' resilience in the face of their peers' deaths in service (bar imminent research from Serfioti et al., 2022; Lubens and Silver, 2019). Individuals will also vary in their responses to chronic stress (Lin et al., 2015); some will become more vigilant, some more avoidant under certain conditions. A go-to practical approach for individuals suffering from survivors' guilt would be exercises that offer ourselves a little self-compassion. As we know from the science behind self-compassion (Neff, 2012), if we practise this more regularly in our everyday lives, it will become more available to us when we really need it. If we find it really hard to be kinder to ourselves, it can be helpful to imagine that we are standing in front of ourselves, looking at us as if we were another person or friend about whom we care. A question which might be useful at times is: 'If you were your own best friend, would you sack you?'

Gratitude

Gratitude is now known to be one of the most powerful cognitive resilience tools out there (e.g. Cregg and Cheavens, 2021). Appreciating a positive experience doesn't need to be a cognitive or even spiritual thing. There doesn't even need to be a recipient for the gratitude (someone or some being to whom you are saying thank you) – all the brain needs is for the sentiment to be there. Science shows (Fox et al., 2015) that the most advanced part of our brain, the prefrontal cortex, activates when we feel gratitude. This area of the brain is the seat of our executive function, decision-making and ability to act smartly with compassion. One reasonable explanation for this is that by being grateful for something, we have something we value to be grateful for. It could be that this sense of 'having' or 'receiving' (i.e., being resourced in some way) accompanied perhaps by a feeling of connection (be it to a person or indeed a force, such as justice or karma or even plain old cause and effect) is a combination that brings resilience. We have a chance to feel resourced and connected to something with strength if we are feeling grateful. So, how can we put this into practice? Do we need to be grateful for everything all the time, even if we feel rotten or hard done by? No.

Gratitude is powerful and needs to be implemented skilfully. There are many guided practices available online to start us off, but perhaps a good way to begin is in the basic, most physical sense. A tangible way of feeling the benefit of gratitude practice is to try a somatic practice. Another, very simple way of getting our brains used to acknowledging positive components to life, and growing that sense of being resourced or connected, is to note three things (people, actions, sensory experiences or ideas) for which we are grateful at the end of each day. It is advisable to start off lightly, perhaps with a bit of humour so we are not self-conscious or distracted by feeling pious. One could feel grateful, for example, for the fact that you noticed someone wearing odd socks, which cracked you up, or that your favourite meal was just how you like it, or for the song on the radio at work just when you needed it most. Working up to more substantial things can come with time.

Compassion

Compassion can work similarly to gratitude in so far as it can be very empowering, even though it may seem at first glance as something that has the risk of making us feel vulnerable. The reason for this is very much borne out in neuroscience (Burgos-Robles et al., 2017). It has long been recognised that the prefrontal cortex (where compassion emanates from in our brain) competes for resources with our limbic system (where we contextualise the amygdala's fear response with the hippocampal memory system). The two cannot dominate simultaneously and, therefore, there will be times when considering others can have the added benefit of reducing our own stress response (Morelli et al., 2015; Seppälä et al., 2017; Rojas et al., 2023; Pérez-Aranda et al., 2021). This means that compassion can be used very pragmatically and skilfully as an arguably selfish way to regulate our threat responses, when we know they are either disproportionate or unnecessary. A very expedient example of smart compassion emanates from work with family liaison officers (FLO), members of the police who support families through times of traumatic loss, such as the murder of a child. In qualitative research undertaken in preparation for a study into trauma resilience (Brewin et al., 2022), one FLO relayed that she 'was deeply moved by the parents' suffering, but [she] was also aware that this was not [her] own'. This is a great working practice of the technique, 'This is not me', to which we have previously referred. Another practical technique is to imagine that when we sense we are becoming bound in another's suffering or that our compassion is becoming too painful to bear, we imagine a window between us and those for whom we care. Through this window we can be there with them in the suffering, see it and be seen doing so, but there is a degree of separation. We can take this further by consciously deciding what we want to do with that window: do we keep it closed? Can it be opened sometimes? Do we on occasion need to close a curtain to regain our composure or look after ourselves?

12

Kindness, Empathy and the Power of Community

The Value of Positive Habits and Rewiring the Brain

'The simplest acts of kindness are by far more powerful than a thousand heads bowing in prayer.'

Mahatma Gandhi, Indian lawyer, politician and social activist

Today, more and more people talk about the importance of kindness and of being kind – something I support one hundred per cent – but what does this really mean in the context of navigating challenges? Concepts such as 'random acts of kindness' and 'paying it forward' are thought of as being good for the soul and providing felt benefits, but why? There have even been studies that show how compassion can fuel resilience in specific occupations and how self-compassion within mindfulness practice can increase resilience. But how can kindness help us to keep going, moving forward and growing, while also building our individual or collective resilience, in spite of the mental or physical wounds or scars we may be carrying?

Personally, had it not been for the kindness, empathy and love shown by friends, from early childhood and every year since, I believe that I would not have made it through the most difficult periods of my life in the same strong mental and (albeit slightly battered) physical shape.

Friends who would not take no for an answer. Friends who kept checking in on me when I couldn't summon up the energy or interest to respond to their calls or messages. Friends who went above and beyond to be there and to listen. Friends who travelled long distances to see me, despite significant disruption to their own lives. These are the friends to whom I owe so much.

While I've never been completely overwhelmed to the point of decision paralysis, there have occasionally been periods in which I was unable to see how to influence positively the situation unfolding around me or chart a way through.

The toughest of these challenges remains that of trying to play a meaningful part in my daughter's life. In the darkest parenting moments, with limited physical or emotional energy to deal with what was happening, and barely enough money to eat, I had few options. It was in these moments, when even getting out of bed was a struggle, that the protective safety net my friends and the veteran community provided, alongside the wonderful companionship of Maia, proved game changing.

I didn't need or want sympathy, but being the recipient of kindness and empathy from a community, mostly many thousands of miles away, was a powerful tonic. Being a recipient of compassion throughout my life from childhood has been fundamental to my resilience journey and is something for which I remain immensely grateful. It has been, and continues to be, a resource on which I draw strength.

What I was not ready for, and what surprised me, however, was not how many people cared, but the fact that those who showed the most interest were not necessarily those closest to me; in other words, the people I perhaps assumed would be there often were not. While I don't blame any of them for this, it did at times increase my sense of isolation, making those interventions that did take place even more welcome and more meaningful.

Even though I did occasionally feel let down, taking a moment to be more mindful of others allowed me to regulate my stress response. Although I am not a neuropsychologist (I am not sure the world would ever be ready for that), I've been taught that this may be because of competing neural networks. In layman's terms, this can be understood in the following way: if I have enough in my tank to think about others, then I have already enough in my tank to think about myself.

Although those who did step in were far from strangers, support from people with whom I had not previously developed a close connection was something from which I drew strength, as well as teaching me valuable lessons about the power of community; lessons I have attempted to take forward in my own support of those who might be struggling, both in my personal and professional networks.

The fact that people I didn't know very well cared enough to reach out, moved me. It caused me to re-evaluate my own networks and how actively I, too, could or should support others.

With the most demanding trials of the past 15 years relating to family, this has necessarily meant long periods away from home, on the other side of the world. Countless Christmases and New Year's spent alone, waiting for contact. With distance being a significant barrier to one's organic support network, trying not to feel emotionally as well as physically separated has been a challenge. Even though we don't know what might happen in the future, we do know that we can influence the present and being open to the bigger picture can help us remain grounded.

I now know, from first-hand experience, that it does not matter how close you might be to someone; just being a good listener might be all that's needed to make a meaningful difference and, in the most extreme cases, the difference between life and death. And the beauty is that it's not difficult. It could be as simple as a text, email or phone call. To that end, I now employ a policy of 'If in doubt, reach out'.

Taking time to remember that there are always others facing far more challenging situations, some daily, is something I try to do regularly. But, as I am sure is the case for many of us, life repeatedly distracts us and gets in the way. So, leveraging what we know from neuroscience, the only way to really build in this type of thinking to our minds is to incorporate it into our day and make it a habit. I've read that when meditation teachers are asked what they find the most challenging part of rewiring the human brain, the simple answer is so often 'making time'. I can empathise with this.

One such family, who I do make time to think of daily, has been dealt a particularly difficult hand. Their beautiful daughter Abigail was born with Rett syndrome, a rare genetic disorder that affects the development of the brain. Undetected until she was a toddler, Abigail's life is a constant battle against the effects of the condition, which include complete loss of speech, limited hand function and mobility issues, as well as increased risk of seizures, scoliosis and problems sleeping. Yet, despite these daily difficulties, she and her parents refuse to give up. They remain some of the most inspirational people I have ever met and, for me, epitomise the word resilient.

While Abigail's parents have found a way to cope with their

situation and have a powerful and supportive community of carers and health professionals around them, what would they do if they were struggling? Thankfully, these days, rather than poor mental health being hidden or something to be ashamed of, it is a topic society now seems far more comfortable discussing openly, thereby removing the stigma that prevailed for decades and opening not only pathways to a plethora of innovative support options but also, even more importantly, just normalising the conversation.

While poor mental health can impact anyone, I have focused my efforts on supporting primarily the veteran community, who suffer disproportionately when compared to the wider population. That said, a vast majority of military and other veterans of service return to civilian life without any issues and go on to lead fulfilling lives, both personally and professionally. There is, however, a minority for whom the mental and physical scars of their service are just too deep, and which continue to impact their lives. It is this cohort that I am most keen to serve.

To that end, I am proud to work closely with both the RBLI as an ambassador and founding patron of their Tommy Club, as well as with Combat Stress, for whom I have acted as a board member for their centenary appeal. Both have existed for a long time, having been established in 1919 in the aftermath of the First World War. Combat Stress' focus is to tackle trauma-related mental health problems such as anxiety, depression and post-traumatic stress disorder (PTSD). RBLI, similarly, has a mental health focus, but also provides a wide range of employment options to veterans and people with disabilities, offers supported housing and traditional care homes for veterans and their families, as well as specialist dementia care. Both deserve greater recognition for what they do.

I am also a loyal supporter of the Gurkha Welfare Trust (GWT), a British charity established in 1969, whose mission is to provide financial, medical and development aid to Gurkha veterans, their families and communities in Nepal, and increasingly in the UK and elsewhere. Without this support, many of the bravest soldiers who have served in the British Army would be destitute. Their work is genuinely lifesaving.

Being able to work with charities such as these, and others like them, is both humbling and rewarding. Having the opportunity to speak to those with the greatest need and understand the challenges they face has been a great way to gain valuable perspective. And seeing the strength they have gained from treating themselves with kindness, as well as being honest, open and vulnerable, is an amazing transformation to be able to observe.

It was for RBLI that I ran many marathons (not least while in Covid-19 quarantine), to highlight the mental health challenges facing those who found being alone really tough and might be struggling. And it was for another charity, Walking with the Wounded, in 2021 that I accidentally ran seven marathons with fellow veteran Brian Wood MC for his 'Ultimate Sacrifice' challenge – running 25 marathons in 25 days – one mile for every British service member killed in Iraq and Afghanistan. For those seeking to find purpose, serve others and be part of a community with like-minded people, getting involved with a charity of any kind can be extremely helpful in overcoming feelings of isolation.

Similarly, attempting a 125-mile route march with a team of six veterans while carrying a 165 lb stretcher – to raise awareness of the scourge of adult suicide and raise money for the charity CALM (Campaign Against Living Miserably) – was one of the toughest charity challenges I've taken on; far harder than any of us anticipated. But the camaraderie and singular focus on the mission and cause made our short-term discomfort worth it. The fact that we were unable to complete the challenge was humbling, with each of us learning something valuable about leadership, teamwork and our individual and collective resilience. But that failure enabled us to tell a far more powerful story about adversity and learning, while still raising a significant sum of money for the charity and reinforcing the power of community. As difficult as it was to retire early from the challenge – on safety grounds – it was the right decision; head had to rule over heart in this case.

Despite the self-inflicted pain of charity challenges, the rigours of my decades' long service have had a debilitating or permanent impact only on my physical rather than my mental health, so far. While I am saddled with several permanent disabilities, I see these as minor inconveniences, when compared to those whose lives have been devastated by theirs. Despite losing around 30 per cent movement in my left leg after being shot, having no feeling above the knee in the same leg following a different incident, along with non-freezing cold injuries in all fingers and toes, as well as damaged finger joints from several parachuting experiences, I consider myself to be extremely fortunate.

I don't know if my childhood trauma or other significant events in adulthood played a part in setting me up to survive, thrive and overcome each challenge, but thankfully I appear to have found a way to navigate through just about everything, while hoping that the most extreme portion of my life is behind me. That is not to say that I won't succumb in the future, given the fact that none of us knows how or when trauma might strike, but for now I am one of the lucky ones, seeking growth wherever I can. What I do know, however, is that gratitude and my inclination to see the positives in everything has been helpful; Buddhist tradition never needed neuroscience to tell them that accepting suffering leads to great cognitive freedom and peace of mind.

The default understanding in society tends to be that the military is most exposed or impacted by trauma due to their involvement in conflict. While my experience is arguably a little more extreme than many, the likelihood is that, on average, only a small percentage (some 8 per cent) will suffer from combat or service-related trauma.

The military as a community may in fact, as a percentage, see or experience far less trauma in even a 15- or 20-year career, than, say, a nurse, doctor, paramedic, police officer or firefighter might see in a month. Given that trauma doesn't discriminate between service, uniform, nationality, language, gender or orientation, I believe we should think far more holistically and inclusively about trauma and mental health and how it can impact those who serve – the military, firefighters, doctors, nurses and other health professionals, paramedics, law enforcement and rescue services – and raise awareness to better support those who may be suffering. However, capturing reliable numbers on the amount of trauma exposures encountered in the military and in emergency response is notoriously hard.

I doubt many of us check if the police, fire or ambulance services are available before we head out on a long road trip. But if we have an accident on that journey, we will almost certainly expect the relevant services to come to our aid. These service personnel are the hidden heroes of our society – the best of us – going about their work without fuss or fanfare, often unseen and unsung. It is for these servants we must think more inclusively and holistically and about how each of us can play our part; finding ways to show that we respect, care and support their effort and sacrifice.

In an increasingly polarised world, it's important to remind ourselves there is more that unites than divides us and that there are millions of fellow citizens serving their countries and communities, often hidden from view. Let's not forget, therefore, those who serve us all. Together, we can genuinely make a difference, one act of kindness at a time.

Although I have encountered some of the worst humanity has to offer, I have also had the good fortune to meet many of the kindest people anywhere, one of whom is now my wife. After several challenging relationship experiences had rather coloured my judgement about and expectations of what is either normal or acceptable, meeting someone so kind has been both a revelation and a blessing. Life is finally beautifully simple and devoid of the angst and drama to which I had become accustomed.

With kindness in mind, I'd like to share a couple of stories of unadulterated generosity from one of the poorest countries on earth, to which I return whenever I begin to lose sight of the bigger picture.

Shortly after joining the Gurkhas and following my first operational deployment to the Balkans, where I witnessed first-hand the aftermath of a society that seemed hell bent on destroying itself, it was a blessing to find myself only a few months later in the magical (then) Kingdom of Nepal, to learn more about the culture and improve my spoken Nepali.

For many years, and prior to my joining the regiment, language courses were run out of Hong Kong. Today, they are taught at the Gurkha camp in Pokhara, in western Nepal, affording students the opportunity to speak 'classroom Nepali' during the day and 'bar Nepali' at night. Annoyingly, for my cohort, we joined during a period where training took place in a small Gurkha camp in the UK, making it a much more subdued affair.

Our two-week basic Nepali course gave us only the bare bones, following which we attended a more intensive eight-week programme that included the requirement to read and write in Devanagari script. Clearly, receiving only ten weeks' training is not enough to be truly confident or competent, so every junior officer was given the opportunity to visit Nepal and trek in the hills, not only to improve one's understanding of the country and its people but also to carry out welfare work for the GWT. For someone who loves international travel and experiencing other cultures, this was a chance of a lifetime. I was giddy at the prospect.

On arrival in Kathmandu, I was collected by a driver from the embassy and taken to the British Army headquarters in Nepal, where I met my three guides (the lead guide also being called Ash, full name Ashok, much to the amusement of his sidekicks).

As every trek is different, I was tasked to walk from Jiri, a small town east of Kathmandu, to Beltar, a large market town to the west of Dharan, in the east of the country. With the distance from start to finish being only 70 miles as the crow flies, it didn't look too bad on the map, but, given Nepal's terrain and the fact that we would be walking only on tracks, carrying everything we needed for a month, it was likely to be more arduous than it sounded. And it was.

The abiding and overwhelming memory from my first visit to this astonishing country was the kindness of its people. Despite ranking routinely among the world's poorest, I was constantly amazed and humbled to see how positive and generous they were. I became aware, not for the first or last time in my life, that people who have the least often give the most: a valuable life lesson. And on several occasions, I was to benefit from the incredible warmth and generosity of strangers.

To make progress before the temperatures rose, we would routinely rise well before dawn and, after a quick cup of sweet tea, we'd pack up our tents and head off into the predawn darkness, stopping mid-morning for our first meal of the day, usually rice and lentils.

Ashok and his team were experts in whipping up food by the side of the track, but on one occasion we stopped by a small row of single-storey stone buildings. Following a friendly chat with a lady who'd appeared in the doorway of one of them, we entered her kitchen and proceeded to make breakfast. On completion, we headed off en route to the next village.

Given the warm welcome we'd received, I asked Ashok how long he had known the lady and how often he stopped there, assuming it to be a regular thing. He was confused by my question, confirming that he had never met her before in his life. When she came to the door to ask where we were going and why there was a foreigner with them, he'd explained that we were walking to Beltar and checking up on GWT welfare projects. On hearing this, she'd insisted that we come into her home and use whatever we needed. I wish I'd heard this exchange at the time as I would have made more of an effort to thank her for her kindness. I regretted that the opportunity had now passed. Ashok merely shrugged: such generosity was perfectly normal for him.

Being the only Caucasian that some of the kids I met had ever seen in person, our presence occasionally generated a lot of interest, which was not always welcome.

Having eaten something that hadn't agreed with me one evening, I really didn't feel well as we started trekking the following morning. But with limited facilities available, to say the least, finding somewhere private on our route was a challenge. On this occasion, I was grateful to be able to duck behind a large boulder, where I believed I would be out of sight. But when I looked up, I was shocked to see a large group of locals staring back at me, while I was still in what can only be described as a vulnerable position. Trying to retain what little dignity remained, I shouted in Nepali, 'Can I help you?', hoping to make them leave me alone. Sadly, not burdened with Western awkwardness, there were several dozen shaking heads, and they all continued to stand and stare until I was done: humiliation complete.

As if the generosity of the lady and her kitchen wasn't enough, another episode proved to be even more humbling; one that left me feeling quite emotional.

A little further into the hills, we visited a village where the GWT was financing and overseeing the building of a small local school. Apart from inspecting the accounts and speaking with the contractors to check key aspects of the project, I didn't really have any other role or involvement.

It was with some embarrassment, therefore, to be welcomed so warmly. Showered with garlands of fresh flowers, I was treated rather as if I was the sole benefactor. Despite offers to stay in the village as guests of honour for the evening, we made our excuses and headed quietly out of town to pitch our tents and rest, prior to a long journey the following morning. Although it would have been fun to spend time with the locals, this was a poor village and I didn't want to abuse their hospitality. It would also probably have involved drinking a considerable amount of raksi (a traditional distilled, strong, clear alcoholic spirit, which tastes a bit like sake) that would have led to a very sore head.

With our predawn routine almost complete, I noticed what appeared to be a light heading towards us. As I packed my tent and sleeping bag into my rucksack, I watched the yellow glow draw closer.

We were about to leave when the light arrived in our midst, carried by an elderly lady with a small, copper-coloured urn. I have no idea how old she was, but she seemed frail. As we exchanged good morning pleasantries, she opened the urn and proceeded to give each of us a cup of hot, fresh goat's milk. After apologising for not having been at the school welcoming ceremony to meet us the previous day, she said she'd learned of our arrival from a friend and, on hearing that we were planning to make camp outside of the village and head off before sunrise, she wanted to ensure that we didn't leave without something warm and sweet in our bellies.

Given the fact that it was well before 6 a.m. and still pitch black at this point, I asked her what time she'd had to get up to milk her goats. She smiled sweetly and rested her hand on mine, explaining in soft tones that she didn't own any goats of her own. She said she was 'too poor and too old' for that. The milk came from a friend's goat.

She went on to describe that her friend didn't (as I had assumed) live close by, but nearly a mile away, on the other side of the village from her house. To ensure we were looked after, she rose at around 3 a.m., walked a mile to milk her friend's goat, walked a mile back to her own house to heat up the milk and then walked another mile or so to our camp to catch us before we departed. She'd done all this alone and in the dark.

To meet someone as kind and thoughtful as this was a humbling reminder that kindness costs nothing – those who have the least absolutely do give the most. As we thanked her for her heart- (and belly-) warming generosity and departed, I am not ashamed to say that I had tears in my eyes, thinking how different the world would be with more selfless people like her in it.

Although our time together was relatively short, and despite coming from such different backgrounds and cultures, our little trekking group became close. The further we walked together, the more my guides opened up, sharing intimate stories of family, poverty and resilience. While they looked to the West with some envy, in the belief that we want for nothing – clothes, food, electronics and other material possessions – it surprised them to hear me say that I envied *them*.

To be able to live such a simple life, in the moment, and to do so with such warmth was, I told them, something that many developed countries had long forgotten or cared little about.

These simple acts of kindness I experienced in one of the poorest countries on earth did much to restore my faith in human nature. They reminded me – because we all need reminding once in a while – that if some of the poorest and least privileged people on earth have the wherewithal and resilience to navigate the challenges in their lives with such kindness and grace, overcoming odds that would break most of us, then we have no excuse.

So, join me in taking a moment to be grateful for the opportunity that every challenge, failure or loss has given you. Try to look past the pain or suffering that you experienced and seek out the learning, the growth and the resilience that came from it. It may be hidden or hard to see in sharp focus, but I guarantee that it is there, and you are stronger for it.

Most of us rarely get the hard things right the first time, so be mindful that you are not alone. When you are uncertain or scared about something significant you are facing, there will be millions like you.

There is no shame in admitting when you don't know what to do or when you need help or support. Quite the opposite. I've been there and know from personal experience that speaking up takes far more courage than suffering in silence. Trust me when I say that you are far more resilient than you give yourself credit for. To that end, be kinder to yourself as well as to others and, rather than defaulting to the safe option, go for the path less travelled. It will be worth it.

Finally, believe in yourself. You have the courage to take the first step. We are in this together.

Onwards!

PRACTICAL TECHNIQUE: 'FEAR VS COMPASSION'

In this final chapter we explored the power of positivity and generosity of spirit. It's not always easy to access this when we are facing challenges, self-doubt or are not feeling on top form. Thankfully, the human brain is wired in such a way that we have a very convenient 'quick win' which is innate to us all: if we feel fear for someone, it can become neutralised or even distinguished the moment we bring into our thinking the slightest hint of compassion (even if it's pity). The only way this will work for you is to try it for yourself. A good scenario to try this with is someone who you feel a consistent aversion to: someone who gets your back up, about whom you can feel your blood pressure rising the moment you realise you have to have an exchange with them. If you bring them to mind now, take a second to acknowledge what it is you dislike about them. Then realise that they have to wake up every day *embodying* those qualities. What is more, there are likely to be many influences over them in the past that have made them the way that they are, and that they have yet to deal with all that. This slight shift in view can take us from a position of being victim to their annoying ways, to a position of steadfastness, and a sense that we are in a better place, a place which is good enough to take on whatever we need to. Good luck!

Science and Thinking

Childhood trauma as an indicator of future resilience

Childhood trauma is well recognised as a factor in both vulnerability and resilience in adulthood. A recent study that focused on students showed how traumatic childhood experience can indirectly but positively predict post-traumatic growth via acceptance and gratitude (Quan et al., 2022). That is to say that if those who have had difficult childhood experiences can learn to accept them as part of their life and make room for being thankful for new experiences, then this means they have a good chance of becoming stronger because of their experiences, not despite them. Given that adverse childhood experiences are increasingly monitored in mental health and well-being settings, it is of paramount importance that they are considered in the context of either vulnerability or resilience, and that there is the potential for there to be a complex dynamic in individuals, whereby they may experience both as a result of events from the past. Studies which have reviewed other studies of resilience and childhood adversity conclude that resilience is a complex system whereby individuals are affected by their genes and their environmental situation, and that individuals need to be taught problem-solving and coping strategies that work for them (Morgan et al., 2021).

A final recommendation is to understand that the best instructor for your resilience is you, based on what you can learn from viewing your experiences objectively and by using the techniques on offer to steer your own brain on the adventure of a lifetime.

To My Daughter

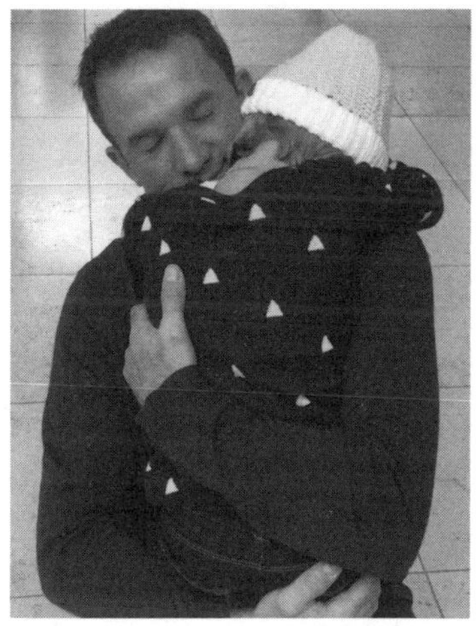

Through circumstances outside our control, time together as father and daughter can still only be measured in days and weeks rather than months and years. Notwithstanding the many thousands of miles of land and sea that routinely separate us physically, you are always with me in my thoughts. And, despite your tender years, the maturity you have shown in navigating our own unique situation makes me very proud. For us, it will likely continue to be an unpredictable path, but, if I have learned anything, it is that the most important things are worth fighting for.

I also believe that it is the balance of all experiences – good and bad – that makes for a rich and fulfilling journey. Even those that result in pain, separation or loss. And, had I not experienced loss, fear and failure in my own life, or never had to struggle and fight,

I doubt I would appreciate life, health, family or friendship in quite the same way.

As a soldier, many times I found myself in situations resulting in colleagues and friends being killed or seriously injured. Even out of uniform I have seen far too many lives cut short, which has given me a visceral understanding of trauma, how precious life is and how quickly it can be snatched away.

I have also come to realise that every one of these experiences leaves a mark: some major, some minor, some visible, others less so.

On several occasions during my military career, I was labelled 'walking wounded'. While this was a clinical, practical categorisation defined by the physical wounds I had sustained, I think that every one of us is, in some way, walking wounded. Because navigating life is challenging.

Thankfully, most physical wounds can be treated medically, but how prepared are we to deal with the range of emotional or mental crises we might face throughout the course of our lives; experiences that leave only invisible scars? The impact of events such as these may be no less damaging or traumatic but could be far harder to diagnose and even more challenging to treat. So, how we approach and deal with trauma; how we develop a tool kit and coping strategies and how we build personal or organisational resilience will be the difference between those who falter and those who thrive.

It is with that in mind, that I offer a few thoughts. Please don't think of these as life lessons, given I am unqualified to offer such things. Instead, view them more as guiding principles that have helped me, some of which may be useful as you map your own course.

My philosophy has been to always seize every opportunity and give everything a go. If it works out well, capture those feelings and positive lessons to build muscle memory. If it doesn't work out as you'd hoped, bank that experience with equal fervour as we learn far more about ourselves in the toughest times, which helps us to build resilience.

Have courage to do the right thing, always, even when nobody's watching. There will be times when you'll likely feel pressure to do or say things that contradict your own principles or values. In those moments, remember that your integrity, sense of fair play and standing up for what you believe in is a strength – your superpower, no less. Harness it, develop it and cherish it. As Winston Churchill said, 'Success is not final, failure is not fatal, it is the courage to continue that counts.' The courage to keep putting one foot in front of the other.

Kindness is a choice. We can all make a difference, one person at a time, so always remember that being kind and considerate to others costs nothing. People may not remember exactly what you said, but they will certainly remember how you made them feel. On the occasions when I've struggled, emotionally, it was the kindness of others – sometimes complete strangers, or friends with whom I was not even very close – that gave me the strength to get back up and keep going. Be someone on whom others can rely, in good times and bad, and know that asking for help is a strength, not a weakness.

Life will be full of events and experiences over which you may have little or no control. Sometimes that may make you angry, frustrated or even sad. It's OK to be vulnerable and not have all the answers, but, in those moments, remember you have a choice. The power to choose your response and how you react to those experiences is precious. Rather than seeing risk and threat when faced with daunting situations, learn to relish the complexity in which you find yourself and look on them as opportunities to adapt and grow. It's all about behaviour and mindset. And, as your godfather Bear says (to anyone who'll listen!), 'Never give up!'

You are a wonderfully kind, quirky, warm, intellectually curious and fun person to be around (he says . . . praying that he hasn't just jinxed your teenage years!). You make friends easily and love unconditionally. So, remember that you don't always have to conform. Follow your passion, seek out the path less trodden, define it and make it your own. Recognise also that the lens through which you view the world will be a product of your own background, culture, experiences and prejudices. Respect and celebrate diversity – of thinking, of perspective and outlook – and always treat others as you'd want to be treated, with dignity and respect.

Although my own military career has concluded, I still have a passion to make a positive difference, to help others and to leave this world a kinder, more compassionate, tolerant and respectful place. Service comes in many shapes and forms, so I hope that one day you will experience as I have the joy of helping and supporting others – the feeling of fulfilment that comes from doing something for the greater good – and finding your own way to serve.

Becoming your father has been the most humbling and rewarding experience of my life. In striving to provide you with the paternal role model that I never had, it has forced me to re-evaluate and prioritise what really matters. Having missed so much of your life, I wish things had been different for us, but please know that I have fought hard for every second with you and the bond we have created. Whether learning to plait your hair, being able to introduce you to the Queen (and you then managing to make her laugh out loud by expressing your disappointment at her lack of crown) or just reading you a bedtime story, each experience has been precious to me. Well, maybe not being your experimental make-up model, enduring a lengthy *Frozen* phase or having my nails painted pink before I deployed on combat operations (which resulted in some very strange looks in the communal bathroom), but everything else has been amazing.

In the pages of this book, I've shared with you a small selection of some of the most instructive, challenging and rewarding situations I've faced, many of which have taken place since you were born. Some have left me wounded and scarred, but each of them provides perspective and insight into my world. I have made many mistakes and continue to do so, but I always try to take something positive and learn from each stumble, as I know you will too, as you forge your own unique path.

The world is complex and, by its very nature, unpredictable, requiring each of us to adapt and learn, often in the face of adversity – the very essence of resilience. Each time we pick ourselves up and dust ourselves off, banking the experience, we are more able to take on the next challenge and the one after that. Before long, you will view complex and uncertain situations as opportunities rather than threats. Accepting that we rarely have all the answers and getting comfortable with that can be extremely liberating.

Try not to focus too much on the destination (something I have been guilty of from time to time). Make time to appreciate and enjoy the journey, wherever it takes you and however you choose to travel. Above all else, know that you are loved and remember that everyone is, in their own way, struggling with something – it's how we choose to respond that makes the difference.

Finally, thank you for giving me a reason to dream and to be hopeful. One day things will get easier and all of this will make sense, I promise.

Acknowledgements

This book would not exist were it not for the support from some very special people, many of whom were incredibly generous with their time. First and foremost, I must thank my dear friend Bear Grylls. An internationally acclaimed author in his own right, it was his encouragement (verging on bullying!) that I must capture my experiences of resilience, so they might help others, that this book was even started. Once committed to paper, it was then my friend Dr Claire York Ph.D., an international expert on empathy and diplomacy, who spent hours with me sifting through the stories to help identify the core themes around which to anchor each chapter. Without this phase, which saw the floor of her apartment routinely carpeted with the pages from my raw manuscript, the book would not have been born. Similarly, having Pru from PAC Copywriting cast her expert eye over my early drafts proved invaluable, particularly when I began to question whether this was a project worth pursuing.

Once I was brave enough to share my work more publicly, Phillip Patterson from Marjacq was an incredibly supportive voice, encouraging me not to default down the path of 'traditional military memoir', something I was also keen to avoid. Thank you also to Harry Scoble, Anna Simpson and Richard Collins, who also provided critical input.

My friend, fellow author and motivational speaker Mark Leruste also helped me unpack some core themes from my life and, critically, made the introduction to Alison Jones from Practical Inspiration Publishing. Alison's review of the manuscript, which ultimately led to the book being split in two (for a first book about resilience, with enough material left over for a second book on adaptive leadership) were absolutely spot on. It was Alison who also introduced me to my literary agent Christopher Newson and his colleague Nick Wallwork from Newson Wallwork Media, who are singularly responsible for securing my publishing deal with Quercus. To Kate Hewson and the entire Quercus team – thank you for believing in me and providing such full-throated support to the book.

I'd like to thank my charity partners too. Lisa Farmer (CEO), Steve Hammond, Emma Nugent and all the team at RBLI have been such wonderful friends and supporters during the journey, not least after I came on board as an ambassador for RBLI and a founding patron of the Tommy Club. Equally supportive have been the team at the Gurkha Welfare Trust, led by Al Howard. My service with the Gurkhas has played a huge role in my life, so being able to (hopefully) raise significant funds for both the GWT and RBLI, by donating my author's profits from the sale of the book, is exciting.

Being able to work with Dr Jess Miller has been an absolute joy. Not only has she brought some valuable scientific expertise to each chapter, but she has also been a true (and very patient) friend. Thank you for being on this journey of exploration and growth with me. Hedgehogs and all.

I would also like to acknowledge Ian, Amanda, Graeme and Chris – expert legal minds – without whom I would not have a relationship with my daughter. Their sage advice and support, generally from the other side of the world, has given us, against all the odds, precious time together.

Finally, I must thank my diverse international network of friends, who kept me going when I struggled to see a way through, and without whom I wouldn't be writing this. The love, support and inspiration you continue to provide means everything to me. I want also to thank my mother and sisters for being there with me on this entire journey, during the good times and the bad. To my wife, thank you for your unconditional love, kindness and support, and for showing me that there is a different way. Thank you also for being an amazing stepmother, as well as a dog mother to Maia.

Supporters

The author would like to thank the following charities, businesses and individuals for their support.

Gatehouse.
Need to Know.

Dr Robin Desmore Ph.D. | Dr Aman Kumar

This book is in your hands because readers made it possible. Everyone who pledged their support is listed below:

(Orange Al) Adamson
Jenna Adikes
Doc Allen
Rob Alley
Joe Anderson
Keith Anderson
Geoff Baker
Lisa Baker
Bammy, Paul Ebrey
Martin Barraud
Nicki Bass
Samantha Batey
Gregory Beattie
Olga Belyakova
Caspar Bentinck
Caroline Betteridge
Clare Betteridge
Vanessa Ast Biller
Miles Blackford
Ian Hylton Blevin
Katherine Boggs
Paul Bookham, Rob Jackson
Victoria Bovaird
Adam Bower
Edward Brandler
Lance Bright
Maria Brooks
Brian Browne
Marc Bryant
James Cameron
Ellie Carpenter
Laura Chappell
Ben Chukwuemeka
Portia Clarke
Andrew Clausnitzer
Michael Coates
Richard Coates
David Collick
Mark Colquhoun
Helen Cook
Giles Cornelia
Miles Courage
Murray Cowan
Sean Crane
Hugo Currie
Lesley Dampney
James Harold Davenport
Col Martin David MC
Will De lá Cruz
Edward Demetriou
Nick Dennes
Ian Denness
Aaditya Devarakonda
Patricia Driscoll

James Duckworth-Chad
Patrick Duncan
Jim Dutton
Irena Dzisiewska
Antonia Edmunds
Phyllida Egan
Max Ellis
Steve Etherton
Lisa Farmer
Angus Fay
Christina Fee
Charlie Fisher
Joanna Flood
Georgie Forbes
Rachel Forbes
Robyn Forbes
FM Frank
Des Fraser
Dominik Freyer
Anders Fridén
Jaquetta Friend
Andrew Garven
Pru
Charles Girling
Stuart Gold
Katy Gordon
Sabrina Greenberg
Brett Grieve
Catherine Grinham
Alison Groves
David Guiney
Junkaji Gurung
Meen Gurung
Ed Haddon
Alexandra Hale
Neil Halsey
Kate Hamilton-Baily
Melissa Harding
Rob Harford
Dominic Harmsworth
Harry, Lisa, Buddy & Poppy
Kweilen Hatleskog
Jeremy Haworth
James Hayhurst
Jim Haynes USMC
Rob Hedges
Patrick Hentsch
Sophie Hill
Stewart Hill
Alexandra Rosberg Hinxman
Hiren
John Hoffman
A Hopcraft
Alexander Howard
Holly Hughson
Amanda Humphreys
Andrew Inman
Chris James
Christopher James
John & Caroline

Laura Johnson
Piers Johnson
Mark Jones
Nathan Jones
Samantha Joyce
Vikkie K
Joe Kay
David Kilby
Martin Killick
Jeremy King
Hugh Kingsmill Moore
Marcus Kingwell
Tim Kirk
Nick Kitson, Tom Kitson
Shannon Kummer
Chris Kurinec
Beth Lambert
Carl Landrum
Brian Lawley
Nigel Lax
Helen Lea
Alison Lear
Desiree Leipham
Mark Leruste
Rupert Lewis
James Lindsay-Fynn
Ben Linton
Abigail Lishomwa
Siseho Lishomwa
Mark Lissauer
Stephen Loader
Jonathan Louth
Alexander MacAllister Freeborn
Tom MacMillan
Maia
Elliott Mannis
Hugh Martin
Tom Martin
Kirsty Mary
Simon Maryan
Abbie Mason
Hannah Mathers
Cristiane Matsunaga
Emma Maxted
Darryn Maxwell
Alexandra Mcclintock
Shannon K. McCombie
Scott McEwen
Simon McGivern
Ruari McGowan Evershed
Lee Mckenzie
Vicky McLennan
Richard Mearns
Garth Miller
Jess Miller
Andre Milne
Linda Monckton
Claudia Andrea Montecinos
Christian Moore
Neil Moreton

Ben Morgan
Sahr Muhammedally
Emma Myrtle
Deep Trouble
Luke Nolan
Jeremy Nowers
Keavy O'Shea
Iain O'Brien
Kevin O'Brien
Stine Lyshaug Olsen
Joseph Ondrechen
Amy Openshaw
Angela Osborne
Henry Paisey
Tristan B Peniston-Bird VR
Rachel Petty
Clare Preedy
Malcolm Preedy
Simon Prideaux
Nicholas Proctor
Neil Rae
Fraser Rea
Keith Reesby
Remembering Calum Downes
Colonel Dan Rex MVO
David Richardson
John Ridge
Matt Roberts
Scott Robinson
Kerry Ross
Harry Rowbotham
Taylor Russell
Christoph Sander
Eduardo Sanz
Lauren Schor
Harry Scoble
Tom Scott
Ed Searle
Sheena
Peter Short
Mike Simmonds
Toni Smerdon
Mary-Lou Smulders
Ashley Sogge
Kiki Ssennyamantono
Liz Steward
Lisa Stitt
Susanne Stohr
Stein Stolen
Hannah Stoy
Thread Studios
Charles Sulocki
John Sutherland
Colin Swift
Andrew Tait
Sean Taylor
Shaun Taylor
Barrie Terry
Chet Thapa
Julian Thomka-Gazdik

Matt Timblin
Charles Timmis
Giles Todd
Lucinda Townsend
Harry Turnbull
Tristan Averroes Turner
Charlotte Tyler & Family
Julia Um
Joy Valeske
Hugh van Cutsem
Stephen Walsh
Vicki Warke
The Warmerdams
Doug Watson
Andrew Webster
Benjamin Wenger
Simon Westmore
Anthony Whelan
Nick White
Jason Whyte
Andrew Williams
Sally Williamson
Anthony Wilson
Ele Wilson
Peter Wood
Emma Wylie
Samantha Y
Claire Yorke

References

Bartholomew, K., 'From childhood to adult relationships: Attachment theory and research', in S. Duck (ed.), *Learning About Relationships*, Sage Publications, Inc., London, 1993

Bhikkhu, T., 'Sallatha Sutta: The Arrow' (SN 36.6), translated from the Pali, Access to Insight (BCBS Edition), 30 November 2013, https://www.accesstoinsight.org/tipitaka/sn/sn36/sn36.006.than.html

Boyd, J. E., Protopopescu, A., O'Connor, C., Neufeld, R. W. J., Jetly, R., Hood, H. K., Lanius R. A. and McKinnon, M. C., 'Dissociative symptoms mediate the relation between PTSD symptoms and functional impairment in a sample of military members, veterans, and first responders with PTSD', *European Journal of Psychotraumatology*, vol. 9, issue 1, 2018

Boyer, S. M., Caplan, J. E. and Edwards, L. K., 'Trauma-related dissociation and the dissociative disorders: Neglected symptoms with severe public health consequences', *Delaware Journal of Public Health*, vol. 8, issue 2, 2022

Brandon, M., Glaser, D., Maguire, S., McCrory, E., Lushey, C. and Ward, H., 'Missed opportunities: Indicators of neglect – what is ignored, why, and what can be done?', Department for Education Research Report, HMSO, London, 2014

Bravata, D. M., Watts, S. A., Keefer, A. L., Madhusudhan, D. K., Taylor, K. T., Clark, D. M., Nelson, R. S., Cokley, K. O. and Hagg, H. K., 'Prevalence, predictors, and treatment of impostor syndrome: a systematic review', *Journal of General Internal Medicine*, vol. 35, issue 4, 2020

Breedlove, M., Choi, J. and Zyromski, B., 'Mitigating the effects of adverse childhood experiences: How restorative practices in schools support positive childhood experiences and protective factors', *The New Educator*, vol. 17, issue 3, 2021

Brewin, C. R., Miller, J. K., Soffia, M., Peart, A. and Burchell, B., 'Posttraumatic stress disorder and complex posttraumatic stress disorder in UK police officers', *Psychological Medicine*, vol. 52, issue 7, 2022

Bromberg-Martin, E. S., Matsumoto, M. and Hikosaka, O., 'Dopamine in motivational control: Rewarding, aversive, and alerting', *Neuron*, vol. 68, issue 5, 2010

Bucknell, K. J., Kangas, M. and Crane, M., 'Adaptive self-reflection and resilience: The moderating effects of rumination on insight as a mediator', *Personality and Individual Differences*, vol. 185, 2022

Burchell, B., Miller, J. K., Brewin, C. B., Soffia, M. and Wang, S., 'The association between job quality and the incidence of PTSD amongst police personnel', *Policing: A Journal of Policy and Practice*, vol. 17, 2023

Burgos-Robles, A., et al., 'Amygdala inputs to prefrontal cortex guide behavior amid conflicting cues of reward and punishment', *Nature Neuroscience*, vol. 20, issue 6, 2017

Burke, B. L., Martens, A. and Faucher, E. H., 'Two decades of terror management theory: A meta-analysis of mortality salience research', *Personality and Social Psychology Review*, vol. 14, issue 2, 2010

Calhoun, L. G. and Tedeschi, R. G., *Facilitating Posttraumatic Growth: A Clinician's Guide*, Routledge, New York, 2014

Campbell, A., 'Oxytocin and human social behavior', *Personality and Social Psychology Review*, vol. 14, issue 3, 2010

Cardona, M. and Andrés, P., 'Are social isolation and loneliness associated with cognitive decline in ageing?' *Frontiers in Aging Neuroscience*, vol. 15, 2023

Ciarrochi, J. and Bailey, A., *A CBT Practitioner's Guide to ACT: How to Bridge the Gap Between Cognitive Behavioral Therapy and Acceptance and Commitment Therapy*, New Harbinger, Oakland, CA, 2008

Cicchetti, D. and Rogosch, F., 'Gene × Environment interaction and resilience: Effects of child maltreatment and serotonin, corticotropin releasing hormone, dopamine, and oxytocin genes', *Development and Psychopathology*, vol. 24, issue 2, 2012

Costa, V. D., Tran, V. L., Turchi, J. and Averbeck, B. B., 'Dopamine modulates novelty seeking behavior during decision making', *Behavioral Neuroscience*, vol. 128, issue 5, 2014

Covey, T. J., Shucard, J. L., Violanti, J. M., Lee, J. and Shucard, D. W., 'The effects of exposure to traumatic stressors on inhibitory control in police officers: A dense electrode array study using a Go/NoGo continuous performance task', *International Journal of Psychophysiology*, vol. 87, issue 3, 2013

Cregg, D. R. and Cheavens, J. S., 'Gratitude interventions: Effective self-help? A Meta-analysis of the impact on symptoms of depression and anxiety', *Journal of Happiness Studies*, vol. 22, issue 1, 2021

Doidge, N., *The Brain That Changes Itself: Stories of Personal Triumph From the Frontiers of Brain Science*, Viking, New York, 2007

Duits, P., et al., 'Updated meta-analysis of classical fear conditioning in anxiety disorders', *Depression and Anxiety*, vol. 32, issue 4, 2015

Dusya, V. and Rodriguez-Lopez, A., 'Humility as a source of competitive advantage', *Organizational Dynamics*, vol. 33, issue 4, 2004

Fine, N. B., Ben-Zion, Z., Biran, I., & Hendler, T., 'Neuroscientific account of guilt- and shame-driven PTSD phenotypes', *European Journal of Psychotraumatology*, vol. 14, issue 2, 2023

Fox, G. R., Kaplan, J., Damasio, H. and Damasio, A., 'Neural correlates of gratitude', *Frontiers in Psychology*, vol. 6, 2015

Frankl, V. E., *Man's Search for Meaning: An Introduction to Logotherapy*, Beacon Press, Boston, 1992

Gesimer, H., Otto, T. and Warner, C. D. (eds), *Impermanence: Exploring Continuous Change Across Cultures*, UCL Press, London, 2022

Greenberg, N., Docherty, M., Gnanapragasam, S. and Wessely, S., 'Managing mental health challenges faced by healthcare workers during covid-19 pandemic', *British Medical Journal*, vol. 368, 2020

Guha, A., Spielberg, J., Lake, J., Popov, T., Heller, W., Yee, C. M. and Miller, G. A., 'Effective connectivity between Broca's area and amygdala as a mechanism of top-down control in worry', *Clinical Psychology Science*, vol. 1, issue 8, 2020

Haines, H. and Townsend, D., 'Self-Doubt and entrepreneurial persistence: How founders of high-growth ventures overcome cognitive constraints on growth and persist with their ventures', *Entrepreneurial Resourcefulness: Competing With Constraints (Advances in Entrepreneurship, Firm Emergence and Growth)*, vol. 15, Emerald Group Publishing Limited, Leeds, 2014

Hanson, R., *Neurodharma: New Science, Ancient Wisdom, and Seven Practices of the Highest Happiness*, Harmony Books, New York, 2020

Hanson, R. and Hanson, F., *Resilient: How to Grow an Unshakable Core of Calm, Strength, and Happiness*, Harmony Books, New York, 2018

Hanson, R., Shapiro, S., Hutton-Thamm, E., Hagerty, M. R. and Sullivan, K. P., 'Learning to learn from positive experiences', *The Journal of Positive Psychology*, vol. 18, issue 1, 2023

Harari, Y. N., *Sapiens: A Brief History of Mankind*, Harper, New York, 2015

Harms, P. D., 'Adult attachment styles in the workplace', *Human Resource Management Review*, vol. 21, 2011

Hope, L., Mullis, R. and Gabbert, F., 'Who? What? When? Using a timeline technique to facilitate recall of a complex event', *Journal of Applied Research in Memory and Cognition*, vol. 2, issue 1, 2013, in Miller et al. (2020, ibid)

Hunt, E. J., Wessely, S., Jones, N., Rona, R. J. and Greenberg, N., 'The mental health of the UK Armed Forces: where facts meet fiction', *European Journal of Psychotraumatology*, vol. 5, issue 1, 2014

Inoue, K., et al., 'Long-term mild, rather than intense, exercise enhances adult hippocampal neurogenesis and greatly changes the transcriptomic profile of the hippocampus', *PLoS One*, 2015

Jaeger, D. and Gonpo, L., 'Self, free will and compassion: shared constructs in neuroscience and Buddhism', *Frontiers in Communication*, vol. 6, 2021

Johns, L., Maharjan, S., Magana, G., Kamptner, L. and Lewin, M., 'Adverse Childhood Experiences and Adulthood Negotiation in Intimate Partner Violence: The Sequentially Paradoxical Role of Interpersonal Sensitivity Among Female Inmates', *Journal of Interpersonal Violence*, vol. 36, issue 13–14, 2021

Jones, N., Burdett, H., Green, K. and Greenberg N. T., 'Trauma Risk Management (TRiM): Promoting help seeking for mental health problems among combat-exposed U.K. military personnel', *Psychiatry*, vol. 80, issue 3, 2017

Jones, M. V., Smith, N., Burns, D., Braithwaite, E., Turner, M., McCann, A., Walker, L., Emmerson, P., Webster, L. and Jones, M., 'A systematic review of resilient performance in defence and security settings', *PLoS One*, 2022

Kabat-Zinn, J., *Full Catastrophe Living: Using the Wisdom of Your Body and Mind to Face Stress, Pain, and Illness*, Delta Trade Paperbacks/ Bantam Dell, New York, 2005

Kanesarajah, J., Waller, M., Zheng, W. Y. and Dobson, A. J., 'Unit cohesion, traumatic exposure and mental health of military personnel', *Occupational Medicine*, vol. 66, issue 4, 2016

Kedia, G., Mussweiler, T. and Linden, D. E., 'Brain mechanisms of social comparison and their influence on the reward system', *Neuroreport*, vol. 25, issue 16, 2014

Keysers, C. and Gazzola, V., 'Hebbian learning and predictive mirror neurons for actions, sensations and emotions', *Philosophical Transactions of the Royal Society B, Biological Sciences*, vol. 369, issue 1644, 2014

Kirschner, H., Kuyken, W., Wright, K., Roberts, H., Brejcha, C. and Karl, A. 'Soothing your heart and feeling connected: A new experimental paradigm to study the benefits of self-compassion', *Clinical Psychological Science*, 7(3), 545–565, 2019

Kober, H., Buhle, J., Weber, J., Ochsner, K. N. and Wager, T. D., 'Let it be: mindful acceptance down-regulates pain and negative emotion', *Social Cognitive and Affective Neuroscience*, vol.14, issue 11, 2019

Kohrt, B. A., Ottman, K., Panter-Brick, C., Konner, M. and Patel, V., 'Why we heal: The evolution of psychological healing and implications for global mental health', *Clinical Psychology Review*, vol. 82, 2020

Kong, J., Kunze, A., Goldberg, J. and Schroepfer, T., 'Caregiving for parents who harmed you: a conceptual review', *Clinical Gerontologist*, vol. 44, issue 5, 2021

Kübler-Ross, E., *On Death and Dying: What the Dying Have to Teach Doctors, Nurses, Clergy and Their Own Families*, The Macmillan Company, New York, 1969

Laborde, S., et al., 'The influence of slow-paced breathing on executive function', *Journal of Psychophysiology*, vol. 36, issue 1, 2021

Levine, S., 'Psychological and social aspects of resilience: a synthesis of risks and resources', *Dialogues in Clinical Neuroscience*, vol. 5, issue 3, 2003

Lin, T., Vaisvaser, S., Fruchter, E., Admon, R., Wald, I., Pine, D., Bar-Haim, Y. and Hendler, T., 'A neurobehavioral account for individual differences in resilience to chronic military stress', *Psychological Medicine*, vol. 45, issue 5, 2015

Liu, X., et al., 'Psychological resilience mediates the protective role of default-mode network functional connectivity against COVID-19 vicarious traumatization', *Translational Psychiatry*, vol. 13, 2023

Livingstone, J. A., 'Metacognition: An overview', ERIC Resource Center, 2003

Lombardo, T., 'The evolution and psychology of future consciousness', *Journal of Futures Studies*, vol. 12, 2007

Lubens, P. and Silver, R. C., 'U.S. Combat veterans' responses to suicide and combat deaths: A mixed-methods study', *Social Science & Medicine*, vol. 236, 2019

Markman, J. D., Soeprono, T. M., Combs, H. L. and Cosgrove, E. M., 'Medical student mistreatment: understanding "public humiliation"', *Medical Education Online*, vol. 24, issue 1, 2019

Matar, J. L., Laletas, S. and Lubman, D. I., 'Mental health concerns and help-seeking behaviors among adolescents in high socioeconomic status groups: a scoping review', *Adolescent Research Review*, vol. 9, 2023

Miller, J. K., 'Navigating trauma: How PTSD affects spatial processing', *Police Professional*, issue 532, 2016

Miller, J. K., *The Policing Mind: Trauma Resilience for a New Era*, Bristol University Press, Bristol, 2022

Miller, J. K., Brewin, C., Soffia, M., Elliott-Davies, M., Burchell, B. and Peart, A., 'The development of a UK police traumatic events checklist', *The Police Journal*, vol. 95, issue 1, 2021

Miller, J. K., McDougall, S., Thomas, S. and Wiener, J., 'The impact of the brain-derived neurotrophic factor gene on trauma and spatial processing', *Journal of Clinical Medicine*, vol. 6, issue 12, 2017

Miller, J. K., McDougall, S., Thomas, S. and Wiener, J., 'Impairment in active navigation from trauma and post-traumatic stress disorder', *Neurobiology of Learning and Memory*, vol. 140, 2017

Miller, J. K., Peart, A. and Soffia, M., 'Can police be trained in trauma processing to minimise PTSD symptoms? Feasibility and proof of concept with a newly recruited UK police population', *The Police Journal*, vol. 93, issue 4, 2020

Miyagi, T., et al., 'Psychological resilience is correlated with dynamic changes in functional connectivity within the default mode network during a cognitive task', *Scientific Reports*, vol. 10, issue 1, 2020

Morgan, C. A., Chang, Y. H., Choy, O., Tsai, M. C. and Hsieh, S., 'Adverse childhood experiences are associated with reduced psychological resilience in youth: a systematic review and meta-analysis', *Children*, vol. 9, issue 1, 2021

Morelli, S. A., Leiberman, M. D. and Zaki, J., 'The emerging study of positive empathy', *Social and Personality Psychology Compass*, vol. 9, issue 2, 2015

Neff, K. D., 'The science of self-compassion', in C. K. Germer and R. D. Siegel (eds), *Wisdom and Compassion in Psychotherapy: Deepening Mindfulness in Clinical Practice*, The Guilford Press, New York, 2012

Neimeyer, R. and Stewart, A., 'Trauma, healing, and the narrative employment of loss', *Families in Society*, vol. 77, issue 6, 1996

Norris, G. and Norris H., 'Building resilience through sport in young people with adverse childhood experiences', *Frontiers in Sports and Active Living*, vol. 3, 2021

O'Connor, M. F. and Arizmendi, B. J., 'Neuropsychological correlates of complicated grief in older spousally bereaved adults', *The Journals of Gerontology, Series B, Psychological Sciences and Social Sciences*, vol. 69, issue 1, 2014

Perchtold, C. M., Weiss, E. M., Rominger, C., Feyaerts, K., Ruch, W., Fink, A. and Papousek, I., 'Humorous cognitive reappraisal: More benign humour and less "dark" humour is affiliated with more adaptive cognitive reappraisal strategies', *PLoS One*, 2019

Pérez-Aranda, A., García-Campayo, J., Gude, F., Luciano, J. V., Feliu-Soler, A., González-Quintela, A., López-del-Hoyo, Y. and Montero-Marin, J., 'Impact of mindfulness and self-compassion on anxiety and depression: The mediating role of resilience', *International Journal of Clinical and Health Psychology*, vol. 21, issue 2, 2021

Porges, S. W., 'Polyvagal theory: A science of safety', *Frontiers in Integrated. Neuroscience*, vol. 16, 2022

Porges, S. W., *The Polyvagal Theory: Neurophysiological Foundations of Emotions, Attachment, Communication, and Self-regulation*, W. W. Norton & Co., New York, 2011

Quan, L., Lü, B., Sun, J., Zhao, X. and Sang, Q., 'The relationship between childhood trauma and post-traumatic growth among college students: The role of acceptance and positive reappraisal', *Frontiers in Psychology*, vol. 13, 2022

Ratcliffe, M., Ruddell, M. and Smith, B., 'What is a "sense of foreshortened future?" A phenomenological study of trauma, trust, and time', *Frontiers in Psychology*, vol. 5, 2014

Rhead, R., MacManus, D., Jones, M., Greenberg, N., Fear, N. T. and Goodwin, L., 'Mental health disorders and alcohol misuse among UK military veterans and the general population: a comparison study', *Psychological Medicine*, vol. 52, issue 2, 2022

Riggs, S. and Riggs, D., 'Risk and resilience in military families experiencing deployment: the role of the family attachment network', *Journal of Family Psychology*, vol. 25, issue 5, 2011

Robinson, J. L., et al., 'Characterization of structural connectivity of the default mode network in dogs using diffusion tensor imaging', *Scientific Reports*, vol. 6, article no. 36851, 2016

Rockman, P., 'Why self-compassion is the new mindfulness', *Mindful*, 2016, https://www.mindful.org/self-compassion-new-mindfulness/

Rojas, B., Catalan, E., Diez, G., and Roca, P., 'A compassion-based program to reduce psychological distress in medical students: A pilot randomized clinical trial' *PLoS One*, 2023

Rozin, P. and Royzman, E. B., 'Negativity bias, negativity dominance, and contagion', *Personality and Social Psychology Review*, vol. 5, issue 4, 2001

Saraiya, T. and Lopez-Castro, T., 'Ashamed and afraid: a scoping review of the role of shame in Post-Traumatic Stress Disorder (PTSD)', *Journal of Clinical Medicine*, vol. 5, issue 11, 2016

Seppälä, E. M., Simon-Thomas, E., Brown, S. L., Worline, M. C., Cameron, C. D. and Doty, J. R. (eds), *The Oxford Handbook of Compassion Science*, Oxford University Press, Oxford, 2017

Serfioti, D., Murphy, D., Greenberg, N., and Williamson, V., 'Effectiveness of treatments for symptoms of post-trauma related guilt, shame and anger in military and civilian populations: a systematic review', *BMJ Military Health*, Epub ahead of print, 2022

Sharp, M-L., et al., 'The mental health and wellbeing of spouses, partners and children of emergency responders: A systematic review', *PLoS ONE*, 2022

Siegel, D. J., *Mindsight: The New Science of Personal Transformation*, Oneworld Publications, London, 2011

Siegel, D. J.,'Toward an interpersonal neurobiology of the developing mind: Attachment relationships, "mindsight," and neural integration', *Infant Mental Health Journal*, vol. 22, issue 1–2, 2001

Siegel, D. J. and Bryson, T. P., *The Yes Brain: How to Cultivate Courage, Curiosity, and Resilience in Your Child*, Bantam, New York, 2019

Simopoulou, Z. and Chandler, A., 'Self-harm as an attempt at self-care', *European Journal for Qualitative Research in Psychotherapy*, vol. 10, 2020

Slavich, G., 'Social safety theory: A biologically based evolutionary perspective on life stress, health, and behavior', *Annual Review of Clinical Psychology*, vol. 16, 2020

Smith, K., Burgess, N., Brewin, C. R., and King, J. A., 'Impaired allocentric spatial processing in posttraumatic stress disorder', *Neurobiology of Learning and Memory*, vol. 119, 2015

Spence, H., 'Experiencing the death of a formerly abusive parent', 2016, https://aura.antioch.edu/etds/278

Strauss, N., *The Truth: An Uncomfortable Book About Relationships*, Dey Street Books, New York, 2015

Suzuki, S., Dixon, T., Smith, H. and Baker, R., *Zen Mind, Beginner's Mind*, Weatherhill Inc., Boulder, 1970.

Tian, T., Li, J., Zhang, G., Wang, J., Liu, D., Wan, C., Fang, J., Wu, D., Zhou, Y., Qin, Y. and Zhu, W., 'Default mode network alterations induced by childhood trauma correlate with emotional function and SLC6A4 expression', *Frontiers in Psychiatry*, vol. 12, 2022

Van der Kolk, B. A., *The Body Keeps the Score: Brain, Mind, and Body in the Healing of Trauma*, Viking, New York, 2014

Williamson, V., Murphy, D., Aldridge, V., Bonson, A., Seforti, D. and Greenberg, N., 'Development of an intervention for moral injury-related mental health difficulties in UK military veterans: a feasibility pilot study protocol', *European Journal of Psychotraumatology*, vol. 13, issue 2, 2022

Winblad, N. E., Changaris, M. and Stein, P. K., 'Effect of somatic experiencing resiliency-based trauma treatment training on quality of life and psychological health as potential markers of resilience in treating professionals', *Frontiers in Neuroscience*, vol. 12, 2018

Zhang, S., Roscoe, C. and Pringle, A., 'Self-compassion and physical activity: the underpinning role of psychological distress and barrier self-efficacy', *International Journal of Environmental Research and Public Health*, vol. 20, issue 2, 2023

Zhu, Y., Zhang, S. and Shen, Y., 'Humble leadership and employee resilience: exploring the mediating mechanism of work-related promotion focus and perceived insider identity', *Frontiers in Psychology*, vol. 10, 2019

Dear Reader,

We'd love your attention for one more page to tell you about the crisis in children's reading, and what we can all do.

Studies have shown that reading for fun is the **single biggest predictor of a child's future life chances** – more than family circumstance, parents' educational background or income. It improves academic results, mental health, wealth, communication skills, ambition and happiness.[1]

The number of children reading for fun is in rapid decline. Young people have a lot of competition for their time. In 2024, 1 in 10 children and young people in the UK aged 5 to 18 did not own a single book at home.[2]

Hachette works extensively with schools, libraries and literacy charities, but here are some ways we can all raise more readers:

- Reading to children for just 10 minutes a day makes a difference
- Don't give up if children aren't regular readers – there will be books for them!
- Visit bookshops and libraries to get recommendations
- Encourage them to listen to audiobooks
- Support school libraries
- Give books as gifts

There's a lot more information about how to encourage children to read on our website: **www.RaisingReaders.co.uk**

Thank you for reading.

---

[1] OECD, '21st-Century Readers: Developing Literacy Skills in a Digital World', 2021, https://www.oecd.org/en/publications/21st-century-readers_a83d84cb-en.html

[2] National Literacy Trust, 'Book Ownership in 2024', November 2024, https://literacytrust.org.uk/research-services/research-reports/book-ownership-in-2024